Gooseberry patch

From our Kitchen to Yours

Smart & Easy
Meal Planning

Delicious recipes and complete menus
for every meal

To cooks everywhere who want to create easy & delicious meals for their family & friends.

Gooseberry Patch
An imprint of Globe Pequot
246 Goose Lane
Guilford, CT 06437

www.gooseberrypatch.com
1 800 854 6673

....

Do you have a tried & true recipe... tip, craft or memory that you'd like to see featured in a **Gooseberry Patch** cookbook? Visit our website at www.gooseberrypatch.com and follow the easy steps to submit your favorite family recipe.

Or send them to us at:
Gooseberry Patch
PO Box 812
Columbus, OH 43216-0812

Don't forget to include the number of servings your recipe makes, plus your name, address, phone number and email address. If we select your recipe, your name will appear right along with it... and you'll receive a FREE copy of the book!

CONTENTS

Meal Planning Made Easy

What is Meal Planning? An easy answer to that question might be that you are planning your meals ahead of time rather than scrambling to come up with something when everyone is hungry. With just a little planning, your meal time can be pleasant and fulfilling and you can relax knowing that you have everything under control. Before you start planning your meals and menus consider these things:

Preferences: Know your family's likes and dislikes and decide if you want to cook "outside the box" to offer your family a few new flavors. If your family only seems to like certain types of food, it might be a good idea to try a new recipe or combination of foods once in awhile. For example, sandwiches don't have to be made with ordinary bread. Try whole-grain pita rounds or tortilla wraps for a tasty change.

Nutrition: How important is it to provide a balance of food and good nutrition when you are planning your meals? For most families, this is very important. Try to include something from each of the five food groups at each meal, or at least each day: Fruits, Vegetables, Dairy, Protein and Grains. If someone in your family has special dietary concerns, become familiar with substitutions such as gluten-free or dairy-free products available.

Time: Even if you plan ahead, some days are just busier than others. If you know your schedule for the week, plan the simpler meals for those busiest days or choose a slow-cooker recipe if you plan to be gone all day.

Budget: If you are on a fixed budget or just like to budget your food costs, plan how much you have to spend each week and stick to it. Check out the supermarket specials and take the time to shop those special prices.

Be Flexible and Realistic: Even if you plan on having a complete meal every night of the week, be flexible if things change. Ordering a pizza and having it delivered may be the best choice if a ball practice runs late or you forgot to get the frozen casserole out of the freezer in time to bake it.

Have Everyone to Pitch in:
You may be the one that has planned the meals, but enlist the entire family to help get the meal together. Younger children can tear lettuce for salad...older kids can measure, chop, stir and maybe even help with meal planning and shopping.

Shopping for Ingredients:
Choosing the right ingredients for the recipes you have chosen can be enjoyable if you are not rushed. Set aside a time when you can shop for ingredients without hurrying or on a tight schedule.

Keep Your Pantry Stocked:
With a well-stocked pantry, hearty meals are just a few minutes away. Quick-cooking thin spaghetti, ramen noodles and instant rice can become the basis for all kinds of hearty dishes. They're handy for "stretching" a dish for extra guests too. Canned chicken and tuna are useful for cooking up casseroles, soups, salads, sandwich fillings...the possibilities are endless.

Tips and Tricks

Here are some smart tips and easy tricks to make meal planning and meal preparation a piece of cake.

- Buy precut veggies like broccoli flowerets, green pepper strips and sliced onion from the supermarket's salad bar. Bags of shredded coleslaw mix are time-savers too.

- Speed up supper...the night before, take just a few minutes to double-check that you have all the ingredients on hand.

- Move frozen meat into the fridge to thaw overnight. Fresh meat can be sliced or chopped ahead of time.

- If dinner includes rice or pasta, put the water on to boil before doing anything else.

- Whenever you make a favorite recipe, why not cook up a little extra meat, pasta or rice and refrigerate it? Later, the reserved ingredient will become the start of a different, family-pleasing dish.

- Label plan-over ingredients before refrigerating, so they won't become snacks instead. Cubed cheese, veggies and fruit labeled "OK for Snacking" are sure to tame appetites.

- Extra ground beef is tasty in so many easy recipes...tacos, chili and casseroles to name a few! Brown 3 or 4 pounds at a time, divide it into plastic zipping bags and refrigerate or freeze for future use.

- Baked ham and roast turkey breast are holiday favorites... why not enjoy them year 'round? Sliced or cubed, they're delicious in noodle bakes, hearty sandwiches and oh-so-many other ways.

- Grilled chicken is delicious in lots of simple dishes too, so be sure to slip a few extra pieces onto the grill. If you are really in a hurry, purchase a deli chicken for the cooked chicken in your recipe.

- The supermarket deli is oh-so-handy for flavorful ready-to-eat turkey, ham, chicken and beef... cheese too. Order it sliced as thin as you like or have it sliced thick so you can cube or dice it.

- Canned beans and diced tomatoes are delicious and nutritious in hearty soups and chili...they even come already seasoned! Mushrooms, olives and roasted red peppers are flavorful additions too. Keep plenty on hand.

- Stock up on refrigerated biscuits for fresh-baked bread anytime... dress up with herbs and garlic powder or even flatten for tasty mini pizzas.

- Stock up on a variety of flavorful salad dressings and zingy condiments...they can give salads and sandwiches extra zip with no extra effort.

- Keep shredded cheese on hand in the fridge...almost anything tastes yummier with cheese on top!

CHAPTER ONE

ONE-STOP
Shopping

**4 WEEKS
20 RECIPES**

Yummy Blue Cheese Burgers, page 14

Firecracker Grilled Salmon, page 30

ONE-STOP
Shopping

Bacony Chicken **Asian Chicken Salad**
Salmon Patties **Yummy Blue Cheese Burgers**
Lemony Pork Piccata

Stock up for a week's worth of tasty meals in a single supermarket trip! Going to the grocery store takes valuable time. If you can purchase ingredients for more than one recipe when you shop, you'll have more time to enjoy those recipes with your family. In this chapter you'll find 4 weeks of recipes with 5 recipes each week. We give you your grocery list and pantry items to have on hand. So breeze down those grocery aisles and then go home knowing you have everything you need for great weeknight meals.

Check Your Pantry

- olive oil
- butter
- salt & pepper
- all-purpose flour
- sugar
- eggs
- mayonnaise
- vinegar
- sherry or chicken broth
- minced garlic
- dried parsley
- dried basil
- dried rosemary
- dried tarragon
- lemon-pepper seasoning
- Optional: flavor enhancer
- round buttery crackers

Shopping List

- 8 to 9 boneless, skinless chicken breasts
- 2 lbs. ground beef
- 1-lb. pork tenderloin
- 1/2 lb. bacon
- 8-oz. pkg. shredded Cheddar cheese
- 4-oz. container blue cheese
- 6-oz. container plain yogurt
- 1/2 pt. half-and-half
- 1 head lettuce
- 1 bunch green onions
- 2 onions
- 1 cucumber
- 8-oz. pkg. sliced mushrooms
- 1/4 lb. snow peas
- 2 lemons
- 15-1/2 oz. can salmon
- 3-oz. jar capers
- poppy seed
- Cajun seasoning mix
- 2 T. slivered almonds
- 5-oz. can chow mein noodles
- 6 English muffins
- 6 kaiser rolls

Tammy Rowe, Bellevue, OH

Asian Chicken Salad

For some variety, make lettuce wraps using these same ingredients. Separate the lettuce into large leaves, layer with toppings and drizzle with dressing...wrap and eat!

Makes 4 servings

1 head lettuce, shredded
2 to 3 boneless, skinless chicken breasts, cooked
    and shredded
1/2 c. snow peas
1 bunch green onions, chopped
2 T. slivered almonds
5-oz. can chow mein noodles
2 T. poppy seed

Combine all ingredients in a large salad bowl. Pour dressing over top and toss well. Serve immediately.

DRESSING:
1/4 c. vinegar
2 T. sugar
1/2 t. salt
1/2 t. pepper

Whisk ingredients together until well combined.

★ GROCERY SHOPPING TIP ★ **Try to** purchase produce when in season. It will be fresher and studies show that fresher produce contains more nutrients.

Asian Chicken Salad

Annette Ingram, Grand Rapids, MI

Bacony Chicken

Choose hickory-smoked bacon for extra flavor.

Serves 6

6 slices bacon, crisply cooked,
    crumbled and drippings reserved
1 T. butter
1 T. olive oil
6 boneless, skinless chicken breasts
1 onion, chopped
3 cloves garlic, minced
1/2 t. salt
1/8 t. pepper
1-1/2 c. shredded Cheddar cheese

Combine reserved drippings, butter and oil in a skillet over medium heat. Add chicken and cook, turning once, until no longer pink. Remove chicken from skillet; arrange in an ungreased 13"x9" baking pan. Set aside. Add onion and garlic to skillet; cook until onion is soft. Stir in salt, pepper and crumbled bacon. Spoon onion mixture over chicken; sprinkle with cheese. Bake at 350 degrees for 10 to 15 minutes, until cheese is melted.

Lynn Daniel, Portage, MI

Yummy Blue Cheese Burgers

These mouthwatering burgers will be a hit at your next cookout.

Serves 6

2 lbs. ground beef
Cajun seasoning to taste
1 c. half-and-half
1 clove garlic, finely minced
1 t. dried rosemary
1 t. dried basil
4-oz. container crumbled
    blue cheese
6 kaiser rolls, split, toasted
    and buttered
Optional: sliced red onion, butter

Form ground beef into 6 patties; sprinkle with Cajun seasoning to taste. Grill to desired doneness. Combine half-and-half, garlic and herbs in a saucepan. Bring to a boil; simmer until thickened and reduced by half. Add blue cheese; stir just until melted. Place burgers on rolls; spoon sauce over burgers. If desired, sauté red onion in butter until tender; spoon onto burgers.

Yummy Blue Cheese Burgers

Melody Taynor, Everett, WA

Lemony Pork Piccata

Serve over quick-cooking angel hair pasta to enjoy every drop of the savory sauce.

Serves 4

1-lb. pork tenderloin, sliced into
    8 portions
3 T. all-purpose flour
2 t. lemon-pepper seasoning
2 t. butter
1/4 c. dry sherry or chicken broth
1/4 c. lemon juice
4 to 6 thin slices lemon
1/4 c. capers

Gently flatten pork slice portions to 1/8-inch thick. Lightly sprinkle pork with flour and seasoning. Melt butter in a large skillet over medium-high heat; add pork. Quickly sauté pork, turning once, until golden, about 3 to 4 minutes on each side. Remove pork to a serving plate; set aside. Add sherry or chicken broth and lemon juice to skillet. Cook for 2 minutes, scraping up browned bits, until slightly thickened. Add pork; heat through. Garnish with lemon slices and capers.

Carol Hickman, Kingsport, TN

Salmon Patties

A delicious standby...so quick to fix, and most of the ingredients are right in the cupboard.

Serves 5 to 6

15-1/2 oz. can salmon, drained and
    flaked
1/2 c. round buttery crackers,
    crushed
1/2 T. dried parsley
1/2 t. lemon zest
1 T. lemon juice
2 green onions, sliced
1 egg, beaten
2 T. oil
5 to 6 English muffins, split and
    toasted

Combine first 7 ingredients; form into 5 to 6 patties. Heat oil in a skillet over medium heat. Cook patties 4 to 5 minutes on each side, until golden. Serve on English muffins topped with Cucumber Sauce.

CUCUMBER SAUCE:
1/3 c. cucumber, chopped
1/4 c. plain yogurt
1/4 c. mayonnaise
1/4 t. dried tarragon

Combine all ingredients; chill until ready to serve.

Salmon Patties

ONE-STOP
Shopping

Lemon-Wine Chicken Skillet   **Gobblin' Good Turkey Burgers**
Beachfront Crab Cakes   **Chinese Pepper Steak**
Caribbean Chicken Salad

When you are grocery shopping, stay focused on your purchases by making a list and sticking to it. The ends of the aisles often display something new or something in season. Give it a try if you like, but be sure to get everything on your list first. After you get home and unpack your groceries, take just a little time to prep ingredients and place them in plastic zipping bags...wash and chop fruits and vegetables, place meats in marinades and so forth. Later this will save you so much time!

Check Your Pantry	Shopping List
• oil	• 8 boneless, skinless chicken breasts
• butter	• 1 lb. ground turkey
• salt & pepper	• 1 lb. beef sirloin
• cornstarch	• 1 lb. crabmeat
• flour	• 8-oz. bottle white cooking wine
• sugar	• capers
• eggs	• 1 lime
• beef broth	• 2 mangoes
• mayonnaise	• 2 10-oz. pkgs. mixed salad greens
• honey-mustard salad dressing	• 3 onions
• rice wine vinegar	• 2 green peppers
• Worcestershire sauce	• 2 bunches green onions
• soy sauce	• 1 bunch fresh parsley
• minced garlic	• Jamaican jerk seasoning
• ground ginger	• 6 to 8 hamburger buns
• dry mustard	
• instant rice	
• round buttery crackers	

Cheri Maxwell, Gulf Breeze, FL

Caribbean Chicken Salad

Try grilling the chicken on a countertop grill for a different flavor.

Serves 4

1/2 c. honey-mustard salad dressing
1 t. lime zest
4 boneless, skinless chicken breasts
1 T. Jamaican jerk seasoning
1 T. oil
2 10-oz. pkgs. mixed salad greens
2 mangoes, peeled, pitted and diced

Stir together salad dressing and lime zest; cover and chill. Sprinkle chicken with seasoning. Heat oil over medium heat in a large skillet. Add chicken; cook 6 minutes per side until golden and no longer pink. Slice chicken thinly. Arrange salad greens on 4 plates; top with chicken and mangoes. Drizzle with dressing.

★ GROCERY SHOPPING TIP ★ **If you take the little ones shopping with you, let them use the child-size shopping carts and give them a list to look for. If old enough to read, have them check the back of the packages for nutritional information. Then discuss the pros and cons of the purchase.**

Caribbean Chicken Salad

Elizabeth Van Etten, Warwick, NY

Beachfront Crab Cakes

These freeze well...just reheat on a baking sheet.

Makes 4 servings

1 lb. crabmeat, flaked
1 egg, beaten
8 to 10 buttery round crackers, crushed
1/4 c. onion, diced
1/8 t. pepper
2 to 3 sprigs fresh parsley, minced
2 to 3 T. mayonnaise
oil for frying

Combine crabmeat, egg, crackers, onion, pepper and parsley in a large bowl. Stir in mayonnaise; moisten hands with cold water and mix well. Form into 3-inch patties. In a skillet, heat just enough oil to cover crab cakes; fry on both sides until golden. Place on paper towels to drain.

Judy Young, Plano, TX

Lemon-Wine Chicken Skillet

This is one of my family's all-time favorite chicken recipes. It is so easy to make and tastes phenomenal! Serve with steamed brown rice or your favorite pasta.

Serves 4

4 boneless, skinless chicken breasts
lemon-pepper seasoning to taste
1 egg
1/2 c. lemon-flavored white cooking wine, divided
1/4 c. all-purpose flour
6 T. butter, divided
2 to 3 T. capers
Garnish: chopped fresh parsley

Flatten chicken breasts slightly between 2 pieces of wax paper. Season chicken with lemon-pepper seasoning. In a small bowl, lightly beat egg with 2 tablespoons cooking wine. Place flour in a separate shallow bowl. Dip chicken in egg mixture, then in flour to coat. Melt 3 tablespoons butter in a large skillet over medium heat; add chicken. Cook until golden on both sides and no longer pink in the center, about 6 minutes on each side. Transfer chicken to a serving dish. Add remaining wine and butter to drippings in skillet; cook and stir until butter melts. Add capers; heat through. To serve, spoon sauce from the skillet over chicken; sprinkle with parsley.

Lemon-Wine Chicken Skillet

Julee Wallberg, Reno, NV

Chinese Pepper Steak

It's a snap to slice the beef thinly if you place it in the freezer for 15 or 20 minutes first.

Makes 4 servings

1-1/2 T. rice wine vinegar
2 T. soy sauce
1 clove garlic, minced
1 t. ground ginger
1 lb. beef sirloin, cut into
    thin strips
3 T. oil, divided
2 green peppers, cut into strips
1 onion, sliced
1 c. beef broth
1/4 t. pepper
2 t. cornstarch
1/4 c. water
cooked rice

Combine vinegar, soy sauce, garlic and ginger in a bowl; mix well. Add beef strips; toss to coat. Heat 1-1/2 tablespoons oil in a skillet over high heat. Add beef and stir-fry until meat is no longer red, 2 to 3 minutes. Remove beef to a plate. Heat remaining oil in skillet; stir-fry green peppers and onion until crisp-tender, 2 to 3 minutes. Return beef to skillet; add broth and pepper.

Bring to a boil. Dissolve cornstarch in water; stir into beef mixture. Cook and stir over high heat until sauce boils and thickens, one to 2 minutes. Serve over cooked rice.

Brandi Glenn, Los Osos, CA

Gobblin' Good Turkey Burgers

This was my mom's recipe...I'll take these over plain old hamburgers any day!

Makes 4 to 6 sandwiches

1 lb. ground turkey
1 onion, minced
1 c. shredded Cheddar cheese
1/4 c. Worcestershire sauce
1/2 t. dry mustard
salt and pepper to taste
6 to 8 hamburger buns, split

Combine all ingredients except buns; form into 4 to 6 patties. Grill to desired doneness; serve on hamburger buns.

Gobblin' Good Turkey Burgers

ONE-STOP
Shopping

Cider Mill Pork Chops & Noodles   Tarragon Steak Dinner Salad

Chicken & Sausage Skilletini   Firecracker Grilled Salmon

Spice-Rubbed Steak

Check your list for staples on hand in the pantry or fridge. If any are running low, add them to your weekly shopping list. Most cooks think of pantry items to include things often used such as butter, oils, sugars, flour, milk, broth, spices, catsup, mayonnaise, etc. If you tend to cook often with the same ingredients, be sure those are part of your shopping list each time. Be sure to check expiration or "sell by" dates when you are grocery shopping but also on the items in your pantry.

Check Your Pantry

- non-stick vegetable spray
- olive oil
- butter
- salt & pepper
- cornstarch
- brown sugar
- beef broth
- honey mustard
- dried thyme
- minced garlic
- dried oregano
- dried basil
- garlic powder
- onion powder
- paprika
- red wine or broth
- soy sauce

Shopping List

- 1/2 lb. beef sirloin
- 1 to 1-1/2 lb. beef strip steak
- 4 boneless pork loin chops
- 4 salmon fillets
- 2 boneless, skinless chicken breasts
- 1/2 lb. spicy ground pork sausage
- 1/2 lb. bacon
- 4-oz. container blue cheese
- 1 pt. apple cider
- 2 pears
- 1 lemon
- 1 head Boston lettuce
- 8-oz. pkg. sliced mushrooms
- 2 red onions
- 2 onions
- 1 clove garlic
- 1 red pepper
- 2 shallots
- 1 bunch fresh tarragon
- 9-oz. pkg. frozen green beans
- 14-1/2 oz. can diced tomatoes
- 16-oz. pkg. linguine pasta
- 8-oz. bottle red wine vinaigrette salad dressing

WEEK THREE

Amanda Homan, Columbus, OH

Tarragon Steak Dinner Salad

Delicious...a perfect light summer meal.

Serves 4

6 c. Boston lettuce
2 pears, cored, peeled and sliced
1/2 red onion, thinly sliced
1/2 lb. grilled beef steak, thinly sliced
1/4 c. crumbled blue cheese
1/2 c. red wine vinaigrette
   salad dressing
1 T. fresh tarragon, minced
1/4 t. pepper

Arrange lettuce, pears and onion on 4 serving plates. Top with sliced steak and sprinkle with cheese. Combine dressing, tarragon and pepper in a small bowl; whisk well. Drizzle dressing mixture over salad.

★ GROCERY SHOPPING TIP ★ **Buying meat can be tricky. The names of some of the cuts of beef, for example, have changed over the years. Ask your butcher for his or her advice on what cut of meat works best for your recipe.**

Tarragon Steak Dinner Salad

Samantha Starks, Madison, WI

Spice-Rubbed Steak

Pair with baked sweet potatoes for a memorable meal.

Serves 3 to 4

2 t. paprika
1 t. salt
1 t. pepper
1/2 t. garlic powder
1/2 t. onion powder
1/2 t. dried thyme
1 to 1-1/2 lb. beef strip steak
2 T. butter
1/4 c. shallots, minced
8-oz. pkg. sliced mushrooms
2 T. red wine or beef broth
1 T. oil

Mix together seasonings; sprinkle on both sides of steak and set aside. Melt butter in a large skillet over medium heat. Add shallots; cook for one minute. Add mushrooms and cook for 2 to 3 minutes, until tender. Stir in wine or broth; cook until most of liquid has evaporated. Remove from heat; keep warm. Heat oil in a separate skillet over medium-high heat. Add steak; cook for 5 to 7 minutes per side, or to desired doneness. Remove to a plate and let stand several minutes. Cut into serving-size portions and spoon mushroom mixture over top.

Sharon Demers, Dolores, CO

Firecracker Grilled Salmon

We love making this spicy salmon on the grill and serve it with fresh green beans and quinoa. It is a favorite summer meal.

Makes 4 servings

4 4-oz. salmon fillets
1 t. olive oil
1 T. soy sauce
2 T. balsamic vinegar
2 T. onion, chopped
1 t. brown sugar, packed
1 clove garlic, minced
1/2 t. red pepper flakes
1/8 t. salt

Place salmon in a casserole dish. Whisk together remaining ingredients and pour over salmon. Cover with plastic wrap; refrigerate 4 to 6 hours. Remove salmon, discarding marinade. Place on an aluminum foil-lined grill that has been sprayed with non-stick vegetable spray. Grill 10 minutes per inch of thickness, measured at thickest part, until fish flakes easily with a fork. Turn halfway through cooking.

Firecracker Grilled Salmon

WEEK THREE

Jonnah Rix, Marion, IL

Cider Mill Pork Chops & Noodles

A luscious, tender meal-in-one.

Serves 4

2-1/2 c. extra wide egg noodles,
  uncooked
9-oz. pkg. frozen green beans
3 slices bacon, crisply cooked and
  crumbled, drippings reserved
4 boneless pork loin chops
1/4 c. onion, chopped
1 c. apple cider
1 t. honey mustard
1/4 t. salt
1/8 t. pepper
1/4 t. dried thyme
1 T. cold water
1 T. cornstarch

Cook noodles according to package
directions, adding green beans
during last 4 minutes. Drain; cover
to keep warm and set aside. Heat
drippings in a skillet. Add pork
chops; sprinkle onion around chops.
Cook 3 to 5 minutes, until chops are
golden, turning once. In a small bowl,
combine cider, mustard, salt, pepper
and thyme; mix well and pour over
chops. Reduce heat to low; cover
and cook for 10 to 15 minutes, until
chops are cooked through. In another
small bowl, mix together water
and cornstarch until smooth. Add
to juices in skillet; mix well. Cook
over medium-low until bubbly and
thickened; simmer for one minute.
Arrange chops over noodle mixture.
Spoon gravy over top; sprinkle with
crumbled bacon.

Elizabeth Cisneros, Chino Hills, CA

Chicken & Sausage Skilletini

I like to make this on weeknights for a
special meal together.

Serves 4 to 6

2 boneless, skinless chicken breasts,
  cubed
1/2 lb. spicy ground pork sausage
1 red onion, thinly sliced
2 cloves garlic, minced
14-1/2 oz. can diced tomatoes
1 red pepper, sliced
3 T. brown sugar, packed
1 t. dried basil
1/2 t. dried oregano
1/8 t. salt
1/8 t. pepper
16-oz. pkg. linguine pasta, cooked
Optional: fresh oregano leaves

Heat oil in a large skillet over
medium heat. Add chicken, sausage,
onion and garlic; cook until juices
run clear when chicken is pierced.
Add tomatoes, red pepper, brown
sugar, basil, oregano, salt and pepper;
simmer 5 minutes. Add cooked pasta
and simmer an additional 5 minutes.
Garnish with oregano, if desired.

Chicken & Sausage Skilletini

ONE-STOP
Shopping

Steak & Blue Cheese Quesadilla Salad   **Smothered Chicken**
Smokin' Hot Grilled-Cheese   **Cheeseburger Bake**
Sandwiches   **Shrimp & Mushroom Fettuccine**

Don't go grocery shopping on an empty stomach! A light snack before you shop will make it easy for you to buy just the items you need. Understand how the grocery store is laid out and you will make wise choices. The healthiest foods for you to buy are usually around the perimeter of the store. If you could shop the outer rim, you'd be choosing fresh fruits and vegetable, meat and dairy products. The center aisle usually has the packaged and processed foods, candies, soda and snack foods.

Check Your Pantry	Shopping List
● non-stick vegetable spray	● 4 boneless, skinless chicken breasts
● oil	● 1 lb. ground beef
● butter	● 1/2 lb. beef flank steak
● salt & pepper	● 3/4 lb. uncooked large shrimp, peeled
● chicken broth	● 8-oz. pkg. shredded Colby Jack cheese
● Dijon mustard	● 1/2 lb. sliced Pepper Jack cheese, sliced
● evaporated milk	● 4-oz. container blue cheese
● grated Parmesan cheese	● 8-oz. container sour cream
● minced garlic	● 2 10-oz. pkgs. leaf lettuce
● cayenne pepper	● 3 onions
● cooking sherry (optional)	● 1 red onion
	● 2 green peppers
	● 1 bunch celery
	● 4 tomatoes
	● 1 portabella mushroom
	● 1 bunch fresh Italian parsley
	● 1 bunch fresh chives
	● 14-1/2 oz. can diced tomatoes with jalapeños
	● 15-oz. can corn
	● fettuccine pasta
	● 16-oz. bottle favorite salad dressing
	● 1-1/4 oz. pkg. chili seasoning mix
	● 3/4-oz. pkg. mushroom gravy mix
	● 10-oz. pkg. corn chips
	● 1 pkg. 8-inch flour tortillas
	● 1 loaf whole-grain rye bread

Joshua Logan, Victoria, TX

Steak & Blue Cheese Quesadilla Salad

Thinly sliced avocado wedges would be a delicious addition.

Serves 4

1/2 lb. beef flank steak
1/4 t. salt
1/4 t. pepper
1/2 c. crumbled blue cheese
4 8-inch flour tortillas
1 head lettuce, torn
1 c. red onion, sliced
2 tomatoes, cut into 8 wedges each
favorite salad dressing to taste

Sprinkle steak with salt and pepper. Grill steak over a medium-hot grill for about 4 minutes on each side, or until done. Let stand for 5 minutes. Thinly slice steak diagonally across the grain; set aside. Sprinkle 1/4 cup cheese evenly over each of 2 tortillas. Divide steak evenly over cheese; top with remaining tortillas. Heat a lightly greased skillet over medium heat; cook quesadillas 4 minutes on each side, or until golden. Remove quesadillas from skillet; cut each into 8 wedges. Combine lettuce, onion and tomatoes in a large bowl; drizzle with dressing and toss well. Divide salad evenly among 4 plates; top each serving with 4 wedges.

★ GROCERY SHOPPING TIP ★ **Choose products such as whole-grain tortillas and breads. Your family will love them and you will be providing more nutrition in each bite.**

Steak & Blue Cheese Quesadilla Salad

Tori Willis, Champaign, IL

Smothered Chicken

Serve with mashed potatoes...pure comfort food!

Makes 4 servings

1 T. oil
1/4 c. onion, finely chopped
1/4 c. green pepper, finely chopped
1/4 c. celery, finely chopped
1 lb. boneless, skinless chicken
    breasts or thighs
3/4-oz. pkg. mushroom gravy mix
12-oz. can evaporated milk

Heat oil in a skillet. Sauté all vegetables over medium-high heat for 2 minutes, or until crisp-tender. Add chicken; cook for 6 to 7 minutes per side until golden. Blend together gravy mix and milk; stir into skillet. Bring to a boil; reduce heat, cover and simmer for 15 minutes, until chicken juices run clear. To serve, spoon gravy from pan over chicken.

Judy Bailey, Des Moines, IA

Smokin' Hot Grilled-Cheese Sandwiches

We love grilled cheese, but I like to give my family healthy choices. This is a great combination of flavors and a little more healthy than the usual grilled cheese.

Makes 4 sandwiches

8 slices whole-grain rye bread
3 t. butter, softened and divided
2 tomatoes, sliced
1/4 lb. Pepper Jack cheese, sliced
1 green pepper, sliced

Spread 4 slices bread on one side with half the butter. Top with tomato, cheese, green pepper and another slice of bread; spread remaining butter on outside of sandwiches. Heat a large skillet over medium heat. Cook sandwiches for 2 to 3 minutes, until bread is golden and cheese begins to melt. Turn over; press down slightly with a spatula. Cook until golden.

Smokin' Hot Grilled-Cheese Sandwiches

WEEK FOUR

Diana Chaney, Olathe, KS

Shrimp & Mushroom Fettuccine

I like to keep frozen packages of peeled, uncooked shrimp on hand for quick, delicious meals...just thaw according to package directions.

Serves 4

1 T. olive oil
1 portabella mushroom, sliced
1 c. onion, finely chopped
1/4 c. fresh Italian parsley, chopped
1/4 t. salt
1 clove garlic, minced
1 c. chicken broth
1/4 c. sherry or chicken broth
1 lb. uncooked large shrimp, peeled
   and cleaned
8-oz. pkg. fettuccine pasta, cooked
1/2 c. grated Parmesan cheese
1 T. fresh chives, chopped

Heat oil in a large saucepan over medium-high heat. Add mushroom, onion, parsley, salt and garlic; sauté for 4 minutes, or until mushroom releases moisture, stirring frequently. Stir in broth, sherry or broth and shrimp; bring to a boil. Add cooked fettuccine; cook for 3 minutes, or until shrimp turn pink, tossing to combine. Sprinkle with cheese and chives.

Jennifer Williams, Los Angeles, CA

Cheeseburger Bake

This hearty meal is great after a long day of work and errands...so filling.

Serves 4

8-oz. tube refrigerated crescent rolls
1 lb. ground beef
1-1/4 oz. pkg. taco seasoning mix
15-oz. can tomato sauce
2 c. shredded Cheddar cheese
Garnish: chopped green onions

Unroll crescent roll dough; separate triangles and press into a greased 9" round baking pan, pinching seams closed. Bake at 350 degrees for 10 minutes; set aside. Meanwhile, brown beef in a skillet over medium heat; drain. Add taco seasoning and sauce; heat through. Spoon over crescent rolls and sprinkle cheese on top. Bake, uncovered, for 10 to 15 minutes. Let stand 5 minutes before serving. Garnish with chopped green onions.

Cheeseburger Bake

CHAPTER TWO

DISH-IT-UP
One-Pan
Meals

Chicken Pesto Primo, page 54

Baked Chicken Chimichangas, page 62

ONE-PAN
Dish It Up

Sometimes planning your meals can be as simple as making sure your time in the kitchen is well spent and clean-up is easy. You may have looked at your pots and pans in the cupboard for years, but never thought about cooking your entire dinner in just one pot or pan. A sheet pan is great for more things than sweet bars. Try using it to roast veggies or cook pork chops. That skillet in the back of your cupboard makes a great pan on top of the stove or for baking in the oven. A large saucepan or stockpot can cook an entire meal. So dust off those pots and pans and put them to good use making one-dish meals that are yummy to eat and easy to clean up.

Make it Easy

- It's always best to use oil or shortening when cooking in cast iron, since non-stick vegetable spray tends to form a sticky, hard-to-remove coating. Bacon drippings work well too. In fact, every time you fry up a skillet of bacon, you're re-seasoning it!

- Make crispy potato pancakes with extra mashed potatoes. Stir an egg yolk and some minced onion into 2 cups cold mashed potatoes. Form into patties, dust with a little flour and pan-fry in a little oil until golden.

- Purchase a variety of sizes of sheet pans. They come in handy for roasting veggies, making pizzas and broiling sandwiches.

- Flip your favorite pancake recipe on a flat skillet. Make plenty because both waffles and pancakes can be frozen in plastic freezer bags for up to a month. Reheat them in a toaster for a hearty, quick weekday breakfast.

- Fast skillet and one-pan meals are perfect for busy families. Choose your favorite stockpot, skillet or sheet pan to cook these recipes. Then just add a tossed green salad and dinner is served! Clean-up is easy too... there's just one pan to wash.

- A spritz or 2 of non-stick vegetable spray makes short work of greasing skillets, saucepans and casserole dishes. And you aren't adding any calories!

- Get a head start on dinner! Assemble a casserole the night before, cover and refrigerate. Just add 15 to 20 minutes to the baking time...the casserole is ready to serve when it's hot and bubbly in the center.

- Boneless chicken breasts and pork chops cook up faster if placed in a large plastic zipping bag and pounded thin with a meat mallet. Then fry them in your favorite skillet and slice to top salads.

- Frozen vegetables come in a wonderful variety and are a real time-saver...keep a good supply on hand for the tastiest one-pot meals.

Lisa McClelland, Columbus, OH

Tangy Salmon Cream Soup

I created this recipe for a meal that's quick, yet fancy enough to set before company when unexpected guests come for the evening.

Makes 4 servings

8-oz. pkg. cream cheese, cubed and
   softened
1 c. milk
14-oz. can chicken broth
2-1/2 t. Dijon mustard
1-1/2 t. fresh dill, chopped
1 c. frozen peas
2 green onions, sliced
12-oz. pkg. smoked salmon, flaked
Optional: chopped fresh chives

In a saucepan over medium-low heat, combine all ingredients except salmon and chives. Cook, stirring often, until cheese is melted and soup is smooth. Stir in salmon; heat through. Sprinkle with chives, if desired.

Charlie Tuggle, Palo Alto, CA

Chicken Enchilada Nacho Bowls

Your family will love this combination of hot and cold all in one bowl.

Serves 4

1 onion, diced
1 T. olive oil
10-oz. can enchilada sauce
1 c. canned crushed tomatoes
15-1/2 oz. can black beans, drained
   and rinsed
1 t. dried oregano
1 T. brown sugar, packed
2 c. deli roast chicken, shredded
8-oz. pkg. tortilla or corn chips,
   coarsely crushed
1-1/4 c. shredded Cheddar cheese
2 c. lettuce, shredded
1/4 c. fresh cilantro, chopped
Garnish: 4 lime slices
Optional: hot pepper sauce

In a skillet over medium-high heat, sauté onion in oil until softened. Add enchilada sauce, tomatoes, beans, oregano and brown sugar; cook, stirring occasionally, until hot and slightly cooked down, about 5 minutes. Stir in chicken; cook until warmed through. To serve, divide chips among 4 bowls; top with chicken mixture, cheese, lettuce and cilantro. Serve with lime slices and hot sauce, if desired.

Chicken Enchilada Nacho Bowls

Jo Ann Belovitch, Stratford, CT

Seafood Dish Delight

A delicious and elegant dish that's a snap to make. Use half shrimp and half scallops, if you like...dress it up with curly cavatappi pasta.

Makes 4 to 6 servings

16-oz. pkg. rotini pasta, uncooked
6 T. butter
1 bunch green onions, chopped
2 t. shrimp or seafood seasoning
1/4 t. salt
1/4 t. pepper
1/8 t. garlic powder
1 lb. fresh shrimp or scallops, cleaned
1 c. whipping cream

Cook pasta according to package directions; drain and transfer to a serving bowl. Meanwhile, melt butter in a skillet over medium heat. Add green onions and seasonings; cook until tender. Add shrimp or scallops and a little more shrimp seasoning to taste. Cook until seafood is opaque. Reduce heat to low; stir in cream and heat through. Add to cooked pasta and stir. Serve hot.

Jennifer Howard, Santa Fe, NM

Breezy Brunch Skillet

Try this all-in-one breakfast on your next camp-out! Just set the skillet on a grate over hot coals.

Serves 4 to 6

6 slices bacon, diced
6 c. frozen diced potatoes
3/4 c. green pepper, chopped
1/2 c. onion, chopped
1 t. salt
1/4 t. pepper
4 to 6 eggs
1/2 c. shredded Cheddar cheese

In a large cast-iron skillet over medium-high heat, cook bacon until crisp. Drain and set aside, reserving 2 tablespoon drippings in skillet. Add potatoes, green pepper, onion, salt and pepper to drippings. Cook and stir for 2 minutes. Cover and cook for about 15 minutes, stirring occasionally, until potatoes are golden and tender. With a spoon, make 4 to 6 wells in potato mixture. Crack one egg into each well, taking care not to break the yolks. Cover and cook over low heat for 8 to 10 minutes, until eggs are completely set. Sprinkle with cheese and crumbled bacon.

Breezy Brunch Skillet

Liz Plotnick-Snay, Gooseberry Patch

My Favorite One-Pot Meal

Curry powder, raisins and chopped apple make this chicken dish just a little different.

Makes 3 to 4 servings

2 onions, diced
1/4 c. oil, divided
2-1/2 to 3 lbs. boneless,
    skinless chicken breasts
14-1/2 oz. can diced tomatoes
1/2 c. white wine or chicken broth
1 T. curry powder
1/4 t. garlic powder
1/4 t. dried thyme
1/4 t. nutmeg
1 apple, peeled, cored and cubed
1/4 c. raisins
3 T. whipping cream
1/2 t. lemon juice
2 c. cooked rice

Sauté onions in 2 tablespoons oil over medium heat in a large skillet; remove onions and set aside. Add remaining oil and chicken to skillet; cook chicken until golden. Return onions to skillet; add tomatoes, wine or broth and spices. Mix well; reduce heat, cover and simmer for 20 minutes. Add apple, raisins and cream; simmer over low heat for an additional 6 to 8 minutes. Stir in lemon juice. Serve over cooked rice.

J.J. Presley, Portland, TX

Cheesy Sausage-Potato Casserole

Add some fresh green beans too, if you like.

Serves 6 to 8

3 to 4 potatoes, sliced
2 8-oz. links sausage, sliced into
    2-inch lengths
1 onion, chopped
1/2 c. butter, sliced
1 c. shredded Cheddar cheese

Layer potatoes, sausage and onion in a skillet sprayed with non-stick vegetable spray. Dot with butter; sprinkle with cheese. Bake at 350 degrees for 1-1/2 hours.

Cheesy Sausage-Potato Casserole

Angie Womack, Cave City, AR

Mom's Beef Vegetable Soup

After my oldest son got married, he would call and ask me how to make different dishes. When I gave him this recipe, he said, "Mom, this is easy...I always thought you were really working hard when you made this soup!" No more shortcuts for him!

Makes 8 servings

1-1/2 lbs. ground beef
1/2 c. onion, diced
1 clove garlic, minced
2 8-oz. cans tomato sauce
14-1/2 oz. can Italian-style diced
   tomatoes
29-oz. can mixed stew vegetables
2 c. water
salt and pepper to taste
Garnish: shredded Cheddar cheese

Brown beef in a soup pot over medium heat; drain. Add onion and garlic; cook until tender. Add tomato sauce, undrained tomatoes and mixed vegetables, water and seasonings. Bring to a boil; lower heat and simmer for 30 minutes. More water may be added for a thinner soup. Serve topped with cheese.

Wendi Knowles, Pittsfield, ME

Chicken Cacciatore

We love this classic chicken recipe! Make plenty of this dish because it warms up so well.

Makes 10 servings

3 lbs. chicken, skin removed if
   desired
1/4 c. all-purpose flour
1 T. olive oil
1 c. onion, thinly sliced
1/2 c. green pepper, sliced
1 clove garlic, minced
1/4 c. chicken broth
15-oz. can diced tomatoes, drained
8-oz. can tomato sauce
1/4 c. sliced mushrooms
1/4 t. dried oregano
1/8 t. salt

Pat chicken pieces dry; coat chicken with flour. In a large skillet, heat oil over medium heat. Place chicken in skillet and cook for about 15 to 20 minutes, until golden on both sides. Remove chicken to a plate; cover with aluminum foil and set aside. Add onion, green pepper and garlic to drippings in skillet; cook and stir until vegetables are tender. Add broth, scraping up brown bits in bottom of skillet. Add remaining ingredients; stir until blended. Return chicken to skillet, spooning some of the sauce over chicken. Cover and cook for about one hour, until chicken is tender and juices run clear.

Chicken Cacciatore

Libby Chapman, South Bloomingville, OH

Nanny Newman's Chili

This chili was a staple on all the camping trips my late husband took with his mother and sister, growing up. It's so easy to take the cans and the browned beef and onion in your cooler...almost an instant meal when you arrive at your campsite!

Serves 4 to 6

1 to 1-1/2 lbs. lean ground beef
1 onion, chopped
2 16-oz. cans kidney beans
2 15-oz. cans spaghetti
2 10-3/4 oz. cans tomato soup
1 T. ground cumin, or to taste
Garnish: oyster crackers, cheese
　　cubes, celery sticks

Brown beef and onion in a large saucepan over medium heat; drain. Add remaining ingredients except garnish; heat through. Garnish as desired.

Tara Horton, Delaware, OH

Chicken Pesto Primo

One summer I grew basil in my garden and froze batches of homemade pesto in ice cube trays. I made up this recipe to use that yummy pesto. When asparagus isn't in season, I'll toss in some broccoli flowerets...it's just as tasty!

Serves 4

8-oz. pkg. rotini pasta, uncooked
2 c. cooked chicken, cubed
1 c. asparagus, steamed and cut into
　　1-inch pieces
2 T. basil pesto sauce
1/4 to 1/2 c. chicken broth

Cook pasta according to package directions; drain. In a skillet over medium heat, combine chicken, asparagus, pesto, cooked pasta and 1/4 cup chicken broth. Cook and stir until heated through, adding more broth as needed.

Chicken Pesto Primo

Donna Jackson, Brandon, MS

Oh-So-Easy Chili

Standard football viewing fare at our house in the fall. Add some buttered cornbread and you've got a fantastic meal! The ingredients can also be put in a slow cooker to simmer all day on low.

Serves 4

1 lb. ground beef
1/2 c. onion, chopped
16-oz. can kidney beans
16-oz. can diced tomatoes
8-oz. can tomato sauce
1 T. chili powder
1 t. salt
Optional: shredded Cheddar cheese, sour cream

In a large skillet over medium heat, brown beef and onion; drain. Stir in undrained beans and tomatoes, tomato sauce and seasonings. Cover and simmer for 30 minutes, stirring occasionally. Top individual servings with cheese or sour cream, if desired.

Glenna Martin, Uwchland, PA

Chicken Spaghetti

This is an old family favorite. It is a complete meal in a skillet!

Serves 4

1 lb. boneless, skinless chicken
   breasts, cut into bite-size pieces
1/4 to 1/2 c. butter
1 onion, chopped
8-oz. can sliced mushrooms, drained
16-oz. pkg. frozen broccoli flowerets,
   thawed
1 clove garlic, minced
salt and pepper to taste
16-oz. pkg. spaghetti, cooked
Garnish: grated Parmesan cheese

In a large skillet, sauté chicken in butter until no longer pink. Add onion, mushrooms, broccoli and garlic; sauté until chicken is cooked through and vegetables are tender. Add salt and pepper to taste; toss with cooked spaghetti. Sprinkle with Parmesan cheese.

★ PUNCH IT UP ★ For a change of pace and a little extra spice, use seasoned ground pork sausage instead of beef or turkey in this skillet recipe. You'll love it!

Chicken Spaghetti

Jill Duvendack, Pioneer, OH

Bean & Butternut Soup

Autumn means a drive in the country to a farm market, then home to make soup. Remember to set the beans to soak ahead of time.

Serves 6 to 8

1 lb. dried navy beans
8 c. water
8 t. ham soup base
1 lb. meaty ham shanks
1 c. onion, chopped
1 c. celery, chopped
 2 lbs. butternut squash, peeled, cubed and divided
pepper to taste
salt to taste

In a 5-quart Dutch oven, combine beans, water and soup base. Cover and let stand overnight at room temperature. The next day, without draining, add ham shanks, onion, celery, half the squash cubes and pepper. Bring to a boil over high heat. Reduce heat to low; cover and simmer for 1-1/2 hours. Remove ham shanks and let cool slightly; remove meat from the bones and chop. Partially mash beans with a potato masher. Add chopped ham and remaining squash cubes to the pot. Simmer, covered, for an additional 20 minutes, or until squash is tender. Add salt and additional pepper if needed.

Cecilia Ollivares, Santa Paula, CA

Curried Chicken with Mango

I love dishes like this one that don't take too long to make and have a unique flavor. This recipe is delicious and speedy...perfect served with a side of naan flatbread.

Serves 4 to 6

2 T. oil
4 boneless, skinless chicken breasts, cooked and sliced
13.6-oz. can coconut milk
1 c. mango, peeled, pitted and cubed
2 to 3 T. curry powder
cooked jasmine rice

Heat oil in a large skillet over medium heat. Cook chicken in oil until golden and warmed through. Stir in milk, mango and curry powder. Simmer for 10 minutes, stirring occasionally, or until slightly thickened. Serve over cooked rice.

Curried Chicken with Mango

Susan Jacobs, Vista, CA

Indian Corn Stew

My mom used to make this hearty soup whenever our family went camping, right after we set up camp. Nowadays we like it on a chilly night. The crusty bread is perfect for dipping in the stew. Leftovers are great warmed up for lunch the next day.

Serves 6

1 lb. bacon, cut into 1-inch pieces
1 onion, chopped
28-oz. can stewed tomatoes
29-oz. can tomato sauce
2 15-oz. cans cut green beans,
    drained
2 15-oz. cans corn, drained
pepper to taste
2 c. shredded Cheddar cheese
Garnish: crusty bread, butter
Optional: hot pepper sauce
    to taste

In a large saucepan over medium-high heat, cook bacon until crisp; drain most of drippings. Add onion; reduce heat to medium and cook until tender. Add undrained tomatoes, tomato sauce, beans, corn and pepper; heat through. To serve, ladle into 6 soup bowls and top with cheese. Serve with crusty bread, butter and hot sauce, if desired.

Deb Grumbine, Greeley, CO

Deb's Garden Bounty Dinner

I love to make this dish because it is a complete meal in a skillet. My entire family loves it when I serve this for a weeknight dinner.

Serves 6

1 T. oil
6 chicken drumsticks
8 zucchini, chopped
1 lb. mushrooms, chopped
1/2 green pepper, chopped
1/2 red pepper, chopped
1 onion, chopped
2 15-oz. cans stewed tomatoes
2 t. garlic, minced
1 t. turmeric
1/2 t. pepper
2 c. cooked brown rice

Heat oil in a skillet over medium-high heat. Add chicken and cook 20 to 25 minutes, or until golden. Set aside and keep warm. Add remaining ingredients except rice to skillet; cook 5 minutes. Return chicken to skillet and continue to cook until juices run clear. Serve alongside servings of rice.

Deb's Garden Bounty Dinner

Nicole Wood, Ontario, Canada

Easy Pizza Peppers

This recipe is also wonderful with Cheddar cheese. Try adding olives, pineapple tidbits or your favorite pizza toppings too!

Makes 4 servings

1 lb. extra lean ground beef
1/2 c. onion, chopped
salt and pepper to taste
4 red or yellow peppers, halved
    lengthwise
4 T. water, divided
15-oz. bottle pizza sauce
Garnish: shredded mozzarella
    cheese

Brown beef with onion, salt and pepper in a skillet over medium heat: drain. Place pepper halves on 2 plates; add 2 tablespoons water to each plate. Microwave on high for 5 minutes, or until peppers are soft. Spoon beef mixture into peppers; arrange on a baking sheet. Spoon pizza sauce onto beef mixture; cover with cheese. Bake at 375 degrees for 15 minutes, or until cheese is melted.

Linda Diepholz, Lakeville, MN

Baked Chicken Chimichangas

I have been making these chicken chimis for years. I like that they are baked and not deep-fried...much healthier. People who don't even like Mexican food discover they love these. I make this recipe often and I even like the leftovers cold!

Serves 4 to 6

2 c. cooked chicken, chopped
    or shredded
1 c. salsa or picante sauce
2 c. shredded Cheddar cheese
4 green onions, chopped
1-1/2 t. ground cumin
1 t. dried oregano
8 8-inch flour tortillas
2 T. butter, melted
Garnish: additional shredded
    cheese, green onions, salsa

In a bowl, combine chicken, salsa or sauce, cheese, onions and seasonings. Spoon 1/3 cup of mixture down the center of each tortilla; fold opposite sides over filling. Roll up from bottom and place seam-side down on an ungreased baking sheet. Brush with melted butter. Bake, uncovered, at 400 degrees for 30 minutes or until golden, turning halfway through cooking. Garnish with additional cheese and onions; serve with salsa on the side, as desired.

Baked Chicken Chimichangas

Kathy Majeske, Denver, PA

Brown Sugar Barbecue Sandwiches

Need a meal for the whole soccer team? This recipe is just the thing! It's quick because there's no need to brown the beef first.

Makes 12 servings

1 c. water
3/4 c. catsup
2 T. brown sugar, packed
1 onion, chopped
2 T. mustard
1 T. chili powder
2 t. salt
1 t. pepper
2 lbs. lean ground beef
12 sandwich buns, split

In a large cast-iron skillet, mix all ingredients except beef and buns. Bring to a boil over medium heat. Add uncooked beef, breaking up with a spatula; simmer for 30 minutes. Spoon onto buns.

Kerry Mayer, Dunham Springs, LA

Western Pork Chops

For a delicious variation, try substituting peeled, cubed sweet potatoes for the redskins.

Serves 4

1 T. all-purpose flour
1 c. barbecue sauce
4 pork chops
salt and pepper to taste
4 redskin potatoes, sliced
1 green pepper, cubed
1 c. baby carrots

Shake flour in a large, plastic zipping bag. Add barbecue sauce to bag and squeeze bag to blend in flour. Season pork chops with salt and pepper; add pork chops to bag. Turn bag to coat pork chops with sauce. On a baking sheet, arrange vegetables in an even layer. Remove pork chops from bag and place on top of vegetables. Cover with foil making a slit on the top. Bake at 350 degrees for about 40 to 45 minutes, until pork chops and vegetables are tender.

Western Pork Chops

Debra Caraballo, Manahawkin, NJ

Creamy Turkey Soup

I started making this soup when I moved to New Jersey from Texas several years ago. It's been a family favorite ever since! I like to add some extra chopped turkey. A roast chicken (or two) can be used also.

Makes 10 to 12 servings

1 meaty roast turkey carcass
16 c. water
1 c. butter, sliced
2 onions, peeled and diced
2 stalks celery, thinly sliced
1 c. all-purpose flour
2 carrots, peeled and diced
2 c. half-and-half
1-1/2 c. instant rice, uncooked

In a large stockpot, combine turkey carcass and water. Bring to a boil over high heat; reduce heat to low. Cover and simmer for one hour. Remove carcass from broth and let cool, reserving 12 cups broth for the soup. Cut meat from bones and set aside. Melt butter in a separate soup pot. Add onion and celery; cook over medium heat until tender. Add flour, blending well; add 4 cups reserved broth and simmer until thickened. Meanwhile, add carrots to a small saucepan of boiling water. Cook about 5 minutes, until partially tender; drain. When soup is thickened, stir in remaining broth, half-and-half, carrots, reserved turkey and rice. Simmer for 30 to 35 minutes, stirring occasionally, until rice is cooked.

Linda Kilgore, Kittanning, PA

Deep-Dish Skillet Pizza

This recipe is my husband's. He made us one of these pizzas for supper and now it's the only pizza we ever want to eat. Delicious!

Serves 4

1 loaf frozen bread dough, thawed
1 to 2 15-oz. jars pizza sauce
1/2 lb. ground pork sausage, browned
    and drained
5-oz. pkg. sliced pepperoni
1/2 c. sliced mushrooms
1/2 c. green pepper, sliced
Italian seasoning to taste
1 c. shredded mozzarella cheese
1 c. shredded Cheddar cheese

Generously grease a large cast-iron skillet. Press thawed dough into the bottom and up the sides of skillet. Spread desired amount of pizza sauce over dough. Add favorite toppings, ending with cheeses on top. Bake at 425 degrees for 30 minutes. Carefully remove skillet from oven. Let stand several minutes; pizza will finish baking in the skillet. Cut into wedges to serve.

Deep-Dish Skillet Pizza

Lindsey Chrostowski, Janesville, WI

Fiery Tortilla Soup

My family and I enjoy this recipe outside by our campfire on cool fall nights...it sets such a nice tone for the season!

Serves 4

1 T. oil
1 yellow pepper, chopped
1 jalapeño pepper, chopped
1 onion, chopped
1 T. ground cumin, or to taste
3 to 4 T. fresh cilantro, chopped
salt and pepper to taste
32-oz. container chicken broth
12-oz. pkg. grilled chicken strips, chopped
15-oz. can Mexican-style corn with beans
15-oz. can Mexican-style diced tomatoes
Garnish: crushed tortilla chips, shredded Cheddar cheese

Heat oil in a skillet over medium heat. Sauté peppers and onion until tender, about 10 minutes. Stir in cumin, cilantro, salt and pepper. Transfer pepper mixture to a large soup pot. Add broth, chicken and undrained corn and tomatoes. Simmer over medium heat for about 15 minutes, until heated through. To serve, ladle soup into bowls; top with crushed tortilla chips and shredded cheese.

Diane Cohen, Breinigsville, PA

Italian Sausage & Potato Roast

So easy...everything is baked on a sheet pan!

Makes 4 servings

3/4 lb. redskin potatoes, cut into quarters
1 yellow pepper, sliced into strips
1 green pepper, sliced into strips
1/2 sweet onion, sliced
1 T. olive oil
1 t. garlic salt or garlic powder
1/4 t. dried oregano
pepper to taste
1 lb. Italian pork sausage, cut into chunks

In a large bowl, toss vegetables with olive oil and seasonings. Line a large rimmed baking sheet with aluminum foil; lightly mist with non-stick vegetable spray. Spread vegetables on baking sheet. Place sausage chunks among vegetables. Bake, uncovered, at 450 degrees until sausage is cooked through and vegetables are tender, about 30 minutes, stirring twice during baking.

Italian Sausage & Potato Roast

Karen McCann, Marion, OH

Justin's Skillet Breakfast

Sausage, hashbrowns, chiles and cheese...there's no boring breakfast here!

Makes 6 servings

1/2 lb. ground pork sausage
2 c. frozen shredded hashbrowns
10-oz. can diced tomatoes with green chiles, drained
8-oz. pkg. pasteurized process cheese spread, diced
6 eggs, beaten
2 T. water

Brown sausage in a large cast-iron skillet over medium heat; drain. Add hashbrowns and tomatoes. Cook for 5 minutes; sprinkle with cheese. Beat eggs with water; pour evenly into skillet. Reduce heat to low; cover and cook for 10 to 12 minutes, until eggs are set in center and cheese is melted. Uncover; let stand 5 minutes before cutting into wedges.

Angela Murphy, Tempe, AZ

Mom's Homemade Pizza

Nothing is better than homemade pizza!

Makes 10 servings

8-oz. can tomato sauce
1/2 t. sugar
1/4 t. pepper
1 t. garlic powder
1-1/2 t. dried thyme
3 T. grated Parmesan cheese
1 onion, finely chopped
5 roma tomatoes, sliced
1 c. fresh spinach, chopped
1 c. shredded part-skim mozzarella cheese

Prepare Pizza Dough. Combine tomato sauce, sugar and seasonings; spread over dough. Top with Parmesan cheese, onion, tomatoes, spinach and shredded cheese. Bake at 400 degrees for 25 to 30 minutes, until edges are golden.

PIZZA DOUGH:
1 env. quick-rise yeast
1 c. hot water
2 T. olive oil
1/2 t. salt
3 c. all-purpose flour, divided
1 T. cornmeal

Combine yeast and water. Let stand 5 minutes. Add olive oil, salt and half of the flour. Stir to combine. Stir in remaining flour. Gather into a ball and place in oiled bowl. Turn dough over and cover with plastic wrap. Let rise 30 minutes. Brush oil over a 15"x10" sheet pan or 2, 12" round pizza pans; sprinkle with cornmeal. Roll out dough; place on pan.

Mom's Homemade Pizza

Linda Webb, Delaware, OH

Reuben Sandwich

Everyone's favorite deli sandwich!

Makes one sandwich

3 slices deli corned beef
1 to 2 slices Swiss cheese
2 slices pumpernickel or dark rye
   bread
1/4 c. sauerkraut, well drained
1-1/2 T. Thousand Island salad
   dressing
3 T. butter

Arrange corned beef and cheese on one slice of bread. Heap with sauerkraut; drizzle with salad dressing. Add second bread slice. Melt butter in a cast-iron skillet over medium heat. Add sandwich; grill on both sides until golden and cheese melts.

Rita Morgan, Pueblo, CO

Rita's Turkey Hash

This is my favorite hearty breakfast to serve every Black Friday, before my sisters and I head to the mall to do some serious shopping. Add a side of leftover cranberry sauce...delish!

Makes 4 servings

1 T. butter
1 T. oil
1 onion, chopped
1 red pepper, chopped
2 c. potatoes, peeled, cooked
   and diced
2 c. roast turkey, diced
1 t. fresh thyme
salt and pepper to taste

Melt butter with oil in a large, heavy skillet over medium heat. Add onion and red pepper. Sauté until onion is tender, about 5 minutes. Add remaining ingredients. Spread out mixture in skillet, pressing lightly to form an even layer. Cook 5 to 10 minutes, or until golden. Remove from heat. Spoon hash onto 4 plates. Top with Poached Eggs and serve immediately.

POACHED EGGS:
1 T. white vinegar
4 eggs
salt and pepper to taste

Add several inches of water to a deep skillet or saucepan. Bring water to a simmer over medium-high heat. Stir in vinegar. Crack eggs, one at a time, into water. Cook just until whites are firm and yolks are still soft, about 3 to 4 minutes. Remove eggs with a slotted spoon. Sprinkle with salt and pepper.

Rita's Turkey Hash

Sarah Cameron, Maryville, TN

Custardy French Toast

The best French toast you'll ever make! Sit back and enjoy all the compliments.

Serves 6 to 8

6 eggs, beaten
3/4 c. whipping cream
3/4 c. milk
1/4 c. sugar
1/4 t. cinnamon
1 loaf French bread, thickly sliced
2 T. butter, divided
Optional: powdered sugar

In a large shallow bowl, whisk eggs, cream, milk, sugar and cinnamon until well blended. Dip bread slices one at a time into egg mixture, turning to allow both sides to absorb mixture. Melt one tablespoon butter in a cast-iron skillet over medium heat. Cook for about 4 minutes per side, until golden and firm to the touch. Repeat with remaining butter and bread. Dust with powdered sugar, if desired.

Kari Hodges, Jacksonville, TX

Skillet Goulash

I like to serve up this old-fashioned family favorite with thick slices of freshly baked sweet cornbread, topped with pats of butter.

Makes 8 to 10 servings

2 lbs. ground beef
10-oz. can diced tomatoes with
    green chiles
1 lb. redskin potatoes,
    cut into quarters
15-oz. can tomato sauce
15-1/4 oz. can corn, drained
14-1/2 oz. can ranch-style beans
salt and pepper to taste
Garnish: shredded Cheddar cheese

Brown beef in a large, deep skillet over medium heat; drain. Add tomatoes with juice and remaining ingredients except garnish; reduce heat. Cover and simmer until potatoes are tender and mixture has thickened, about 45 minutes. Garnish with Cheddar cheese.

Skillet Goulash

Barbara Cooper, Orion, IL

Pulled Chicken & Slaw Sandwiches

Start with a roast chicken from the deli and you'll be serving these sandwiches in no time! The creamy slaw adds a nice crunch.

Makes 6 to 8 servings

1 c. favorite barbecue sauce
1 c. catsup
1/2 c. water
1 t. lemon juice
2/3 c. brown sugar, packed
1 deli roast chicken, boned and
   shredded
6 to 8 buns, split
Garnish: deli coleslaw

In a cast-iron skillet over medium heat, combine barbecue sauce, catsup, water, lemon juice and brown sugar. Stir well; cook and stir until brown sugar is dissolved. Add chicken; reduce heat to low and simmer until mixture is heated through. To serve, spoon chicken mixture onto buns; top with a scoop of coleslaw.

Lauren Vanden Berg, Grandville MI

Skillet Meatloaf

My great-grandma was very poor and only owned one cast-iron skillet. She made this meatloaf in the skillet. She passed her skillet on to my grandma, who passed it on to me. Now this is the only kind of meatloaf I make.

Serves 3 to 4

1 lb. ground beef
1 onion, chopped
1 green pepper, chopped
4 saltine crackers, crushed
1-oz. pkg. ranch salad dressing mix
1 egg
1/4 c. barbecue sauce

In a bowl, combine beef, onion and green pepper; mix well. Add cracker crumbs and dressing mix; mix again. Shape beef mixture into ball; make a little hole in the middle. Crack the egg into the hole; mix again. Preheat a cast-iron skillet or 3 to 4 individual skillets over medium heat. Shape meatloaf to fit in skillet(s). Add meatloaf to skillet(s). Spread barbecue sauce on top. Cover and cook for 30 to 35 minutes for a large skillet and 20 to 25 minutes for smaller skillets, until meatloaf is no longer pink in the center. Reduce heat to low, if needed. Use a meat thermometer to check temperature.

Skillet Meatloaf

Arleela Connor, Leopold, IN

Toasted Ham & Cheese

Serve these buttery sandwiches with a side of potato chips and a crisp dill pickle, or a cup of tomato bisque... pure comfort!

Serves 4

2-1/2 T. butter, softened
8 slices sourdough bread
4 slices Colby cheese
1/2 lb. shaved deli ham
4 slices Swiss cheese

Spread butter on one side of each slice of bread. Arrange 4 bread slices, buttered-side down, in a cast-iron skillet over medium-high heat. Top with one slice Colby cheese, desired amount of ham and one slice Swiss cheese. Add remaining bread slices, buttered-side up. Grill sandwiches on both sides until golden and cheese melts.

Brenda Rogers, Atwood, CA

South-of-the-Border Squash Skillet

Our family grows lots of yellow summer squash in our community garden. We love tacos, so this taco-flavored recipe is a yummy way to use it up! If you omit the meat, it's also a great vegetarian dish.

Makes 4 servings

1 lb. ground beef or turkey
1/3 c. onion, diced
1 c. water
1-1/4 oz. pkg. taco seasoning mix
4 to 5 yellow squash, zucchini or
    crookneck squash, chopped
1 c. shredded Cheddar cheese

In a skillet over medium heat, brown meat with onion; drain. Stir in water and taco seasoning; add squash. Cover and simmer for about 10 minutes, until squash is tender. Stir in cheese; cover and let stand just until cheese melts.

South-of-the-Border Squash Skillet

Jenna Fowls, Warsaw, OH

Grandma's Wilted Lettuce

An old-fashioned favorite! To save time, heat the water, vinegar, sugar, and drippings in a mug in the microwave.

Makes 6 servings

2 heads leaf lettuce, torn
Optional: 1/8 t. salt, 1/8 t. pepper
2 eggs, hard-boiled, peeled and
    quartered
Optional: 2 green onions, sliced
4 to 6 slices bacon
1/4 c. vinegar
2 T. water
1 T. sugar

Arrange lettuce in a salad bowl; season with salt and pepper, if desired. Add eggs and green onions, if using. Toss to combine; set aside. Meanwhile, in a cast-iron skillet over medium-high heat, cook bacon until crisp. Remove bacon to a paper towel; reserve drippings in skillet. Add vinegar, water and sugar to drippings in skillet. Heat to boiling, stirring until sugar dissolves. Pour over salad; toss again. Top with crumbled bacon and serve immediately.

Roberta Goll, Chesterfield, MI

Roberta's Pepper Steak

This beef dish is as beautiful as it is yummy. I like to serve it right from the cast-iron skillet that I cook it in. Everyone always comments on it and wants the recipe!

Makes 8 servings

1-1/4 lbs. beef round steak, sliced
    into 1/2-inch strips
2 t. canola oil
2 cloves garlic, pressed and divided
2 green and/or red peppers, cut into
    thin strips
2 onions, coarsely chopped
8-oz. pkg. sliced mushrooms
1/2 t. salt
1/2 t. pepper
1 c. beef broth

In a skillet over medium heat, brown steak strips with oil and half the garlic. Add peppers and onions; cook until tender. Stir in mushrooms, salt, pepper and remaining garlic. Stir in beef broth. Reduce heat to low and simmer for one hour. Add a little water if needed.

Roberta's Pepper Steak

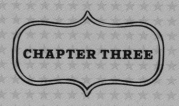

CHAPTER THREE

MAKE IT A MEAL
10 Tasty Menus

Caprese Salad, page 92

Wild Blackberry Cobbler, page 93

MAKE IT A MEAL
10 Tasty Menus

In this chapter you'll find 10 menus to help you plan amazing meals for every day of the week. Whether you prefer a comfort-food menu of fried chicken and slaw, a hearty sandwich with fries or a simple one-dish stir-fry to make in minutes, you are sure to find menus you will enjoy making for your family. Each menu contains all of the 5 food groups: Fruits, Vegetables, Grains, Proteins and Dairy. We have included the main recipes for each menu and in some cases suggestions for additional breads, sides or beverages. We know these menus will inspire you to start cooking and creating the perfect family meal.

Make it Easy

- Sometimes it is more budget-friendly to plan menus based on what is on sale. For example, if beef is on sale, choose a Swiss steak meal or if eggs are inexpensive this week, make egg salad. Look in your supermarket flyer to see what bargains are coming for the week and plan accordingly.

- Theme nights are a fun way to plan menus for the week. Monday could be Italian, Tuesday Asian, Wednesday Greek, etc. This gives a framework to work from if you are looking for ideas.

- Leftovers or not? Some folks simply don't like to eat leftovers and some like to cook to have leftovers. If you are the latter, make a double batch of the recipe you are choosing and then enjoy the leftovers the next day. Or, freeze it and enjoy later.

- Some menu planning might require consideration for food allergies or sensitivities. If this is the case in your family, it might be easier to cook for the entire family recognizing those allergies. That is, cooking one meal instead of cooking a separate meal for that one person.

- Encourage your family to try new foods, recipes and food combinations. Serve a favorite main dish but then add a new flavor in a salad or side.

- Let the children help plan the menus for the week. They will enjoy it and will be eager to try their ideas.

MENU 1

Stacie Avner, Delaware, OH

Dijon Chicken & Fresh Herbs

I love making this family favorite in the summertime with my fresh garden herbs.

Serves 6

6 boneless, skinless chicken breasts
1/2 t. kosher salt
1 t. pepper
3 to 4 T. Dijon mustard
2 T. fresh rosemary, minced
2 T. fresh thyme, minced
2 T. fresh parsley, minced

Sprinkle chicken with salt and pepper. Grill over medium-high heat 6 minutes per side, or until juices run clear. Remove from grill and brush both sides with mustard; sprinkle with herbs.

Dijon Chicken & Fresh Herbs

MENU 1

- **Dijon Chicken & Fresh Herbs**
- **Green Peas & Crispy Bacon**
- **Peanut Butter-Chocolate Bars**
- Green Salad
- Rye Bread
- Sparkling Water

MENU 1

Dana Harpster, Kansas City, MO

Green Peas with Crispy Bacon

I've used bacon bits and even diced ham in place of the bacon in the recipe. Both worked!

Serves 6

2 slices bacon
1 shallot, sliced
1/2 t. orange zest
1/2 c. orange juice
1/4 t. salt
1/2 t. pepper
16-oz. pkg. frozen sweet green peas,
    thawed
1 t. butter
1 T. fresh mint, chopped
Garnish: fresh mint sprigs

Cook bacon in a skillet over medium heat until crisp. Remove and drain on paper towels, reserving one teaspoon drippings in skillet. Crumble bacon and set aside. Sauté shallot in reserved drippings over medium-high heat for 2 minutes, or until tender. Stir in orange zest, orange juice, salt and pepper. Cook, stirring occasionally, for 5 minutes, or until liquid is reduced by half. Add peas and cook 5 more minutes; stir in butter and chopped mint. Transfer peas to a serving dish and sprinkle with crumbled bacon. Garnish as desired.

Green Peas with Crispy Bacon

Eileen Blass, Catawissa, PA

Peanut Butter-Chocolate Bars

Top with marshmallow creme for s'more fun!

Makes 25 to 30

1 c. creamy peanut butter
1/2 c. butter, melted
1 c. graham cracker crumbs
16-oz. pkg. powdered sugar
2 c. semi-sweet chocolate chips, melted

Combine first 4 ingredients together in a large mixing bowl;
mix well using a wooden spoon. Press into the bottom of a
well-greased 15"x10" jelly-roll pan; pour melted chocolate
evenly over crust. Refrigerate for 15 minutes; score into bars
but leave in pan. Refrigerate until firm; slice completely
through scores and serve cold.

Peanut Butter-Chocolate Bars

Cris Goode, Mooresville, IN

Good & Healthy "Fried" Chicken

We love this healthier version of everyone's favorite food...fried chicken!

Makes 5 servings

1 c. whole-grain panko bread crumbs
1 c. cornmeal
2 T. all-purpose flour
salt and pepper to taste
10 chicken drumsticks
1 c. buttermilk

Combine panko, cornmeal, flour, salt and pepper in a gallon-size plastic zipping bag. Coat chicken with buttermilk, one piece at a time. Drop chicken into bag and shake to coat pieces lightly. Arrange chicken on a baking pan coated with non-stick vegetable spray. Bake, uncovered, at 350 degrees for 40 to 50 minutes, until chicken juices run clear.

Good & Healthy "Fried" Chicken

MENU 2

- **Good & Healthy "Fried" Chicken**
- **Caprese Salad**
- **Wild Blackberry Cobbler**
- Corn on the Cob
- Coleslaw
- Milk

MENU 2

Beth Flack, Terre Haute, IN

Caprese Salad

Very refreshing! This is one of my favorite summer salads.
Try it with cherry tomatoes and mini mozzarella balls too.

Serves 6

2 beefsteak tomatoes, sliced
4-oz. pkg. fresh mozzarella cheese, sliced
8 leaves fresh basil
Italian salad dressing to taste

Layer tomatoes, cheese slices and basil leaves in rows or in
a circle around a large platter. Sprinkle with salad dressing.
Cover and chill for one hour before serving.

Caprese Salad

Wild Blackberry Cobbler

Edith Beck, Elk Grove, CA

Wild Blackberry Cobbler

A very old recipe that a friend shared with me in high school. Every year, we pick wild blackberries together so I can make this cobbler.

Serves 4 to 6

1/2 c. butter, sliced
3 c. fresh blackberries
1/4 c. plus 2 T. water, divided
1-1/4 c. sugar, divided
1/2 t. cinnamon
2 T. cornstarch
1 c. all-purpose flour
1-1/2 t. baking powder
1/4 t. salt
1 c. milk

Add butter to a 9"x9" baking pan. Place in oven at 400 degrees until melted. Meanwhile, in a small saucepan, combine blackberries, 1/4 cup water, 1/4 cup sugar and cinnamon. Simmer over medium heat, stirring gently. Stir together cornstarch and remaining water until pourable; stir into berry mixture and cook until thickened. Remove from heat. In a bowl, mix flour, remaining sugar, baking powder, salt and milk; stir until smooth. Add flour mixture to butter in baking pan; carefully add berry mixture. Bake at 400 degrees for 25 to 30 minutes, until bubbly and crust is golden.

MENU 3

Bev Fisher, Mesa, AZ

Grilled Havarti Sandwiches

Now that my children are grown, I'm always looking for recipes that call for ingredients they wouldn't eat. This sandwich is so tasty, I wanted another one the next day after I first tried it!

Makes 4 sandwiches

8 slices French bread
2 t. butter, softened and divided
4 T. apricot preserves
1/4 lb. Havarti cheese, sliced
1 avocado, halved, pitted and sliced

Spread 4 slices bread on one side with half the butter and all the preserves. Top with cheese, avocado and another slice of bread; spread remaining butter on outside of sandwiches. Heat a large skillet over medium heat. Cook sandwiches for 2 to 3 minutes, until bread is golden and cheese begins to melt. Turn over; press down slightly with a spatula. Cook until golden.

★ MENU PLANNING TIP ★ Keep color and texture contrasts in mind as you plan dinner. For example, crispy, golden fried chicken teamed with creamy white macaroni salad and juicy red tomato slices...everything will taste twice as good!

MENU 3

- **Grilled Havarti Sandwich**
- **Minted Baby Carrots**
- **Fresh Kale Salad**
- **Chocolate-Orange Zucchini Cake**
- Iced Tea

MENU 3

Tori Willis, Champaign, IL

Minted Baby Carrots

I make these carrots often...they are so easy to fix and everyone loves them!

Serves 4

1/2 lb. baby carrots
1 T. butter
salt and pepper to taste
1 T. lemon zest, minced
1 T. brown sugar, packed
2 t. fresh mint, minced

In a stockpot of boiling water, cook carrots 5 minutes. Remove from heat; drain. Melt butter in a skillet over medium-high heat. Stir in carrots; cook until crisp-tender. Season with salt and pepper to taste. Combine remaining ingredients; sprinkle over individual servings.

Minted Baby Carrots

Fresh Kale Salad

Carol Werner, Brooklyn Park, MN

Fresh Kale Salad

This recipe goes together so quickly, and is very healthy and tasty to boot!

Serves 6

3 T. honey
1/2 c. olive or canola oil
juice of 1 lemon
pepper to taste
1 bunch fresh kale, torn and stems removed
1/2 c. raisins or dried cranberries
1/4 c. sunflower kernels

In a large bowl, combine honey, oil, lemon juice and pepper. Whisk until blended. Add kale and toss to coat; let stand about 5 minutes. Sprinkle with raisins or cranberries and sunflower seeds; toss again.

MENU 3

Cynthia Dodge, Layton, UT

Chocolate-Orange Zucchini Cake

This cake is so dense and rich, you only need a small slice.

Serves 12

1/2 c. plus 2 T. baking cocoa, divided
2-1/2 c. plus 2 T. all-purpose flour, divided
1/2 c. butter
2 c. sugar
3 eggs
2 t. vanilla extract
zest of 1 orange
1/2 c. milk
3 T. canola oil
3 c. zucchini, peeled and shredded
2-1/2 t. baking powder
1-1/2 t. baking soda
1/2 t. salt
1/2 t. cinnamon
Garnish: baking cocoa

Spray a 10-inch Bundt® pan with non-stick vegetable spray. Mix 2 tablespoons cocoa with 2 tablespoons flour. Coat interior of pan with mixture; shake out any extra and set aside pan. In a large bowl, beat butter and sugar with an electric mixer on medium speed. Add eggs, one at a time, beating well after each addition. Stir in vanilla, orange zest and milk. In a separate bowl, combine remaining cocoa and oil; mix thoroughly. Add cocoa mixture to butter mixture; stir well. Fold in zucchini. Add remaining flour and other ingredients. Beat on low speed until well blended. Pour into prepared pan. Bake at 350 degrees for about one hour, until a wooden toothpick tests clean. Cool in pan for 10 minutes; remove from pan to a cake plate. Cool completely. Dust top of cake with baking cocoa.

Chocolate-Orange Zucchini Cake

MENU 4

Ann Heavey, Bridgewater, MA

Marty's Special Burgers

Serve these zippy burgers at your next cookout...guests will rave!

Makes 4 sandwiches

1 lb. lean ground beef
1/2 c. crumbled feta or blue cheese
1/2 c. bread crumbs
1 egg, beaten
1/2 t. salt
1/4 t. pepper
4 to 6 cherry tomatoes, halved
4 hamburger buns, split

Mix together all ingredients except buns; form into 4 burger patties. Grill over high heat to desired doneness, flipping to cook on both sides. Serve on buns.

★ KITCHEN TIP ★ **Make these burgers ahead of time! Place them between sheets of wax paper and then into a plastic zipping bag. Tuck in the fridge until it's time to grill.**

MENU 4

- Marty's Special Burger
- Homestyle Butter Beans
- Frosty Orange Juice
- Chocolate Chippers

Marty's Special Burgers

**MENU
4**

Kendall Hale, Lynn, MA

Homestyle Butter Beans

Use this recipe for lima beans, too! Serve with your favorite burger for a hearty meal.

Serves 6 to 8

5 bacon slices, diced
1 onion, minced
1/2 c. brown sugar, packed
16-oz. pkg. frozen butter beans
1/4 c. butter
1/2 c. water
2 t. salt
1 t. pepper

Cook bacon and onion in a large Dutch oven over medium heat for 5 to 7 minutes. Add brown sugar; cook, stirring occasionally, one to 2 minutes until sugar is dissolved. Stir in butter beans and butter until butter is melted and beans are thoroughly coated. Stir in water. Bring to a boil over medium-high heat; reduce heat to low. Simmer, stirring occasionally, 2 hours or until beans are very tender and liquid is thickened and just below top of beans. Stir in salt and pepper.

Homestyle Butter Beans

Frosty Orange Juice

Tiffany Classen, Wichita, KS

Frosty Orange Juice

The orange juice and milk combination in this drink is so refreshing any time of year!

Makes 4 servings

6-oz. can frozen orange juice concentrate, partially thawed
1 c. milk
1 c. water
1 t. vanilla extract
1/3 c. sugar
12 ice cubes

Combine all ingredients in a blender container. Cover and blend until frothy.

MENU 4

Mary Warren, Auburn, MI

Favorite Chocolate Chippers

The instant pudding in this cookie makes it extra chewy and oh-so-good!

Makes 3 dozen

3/4 c. butter, softened
3/4 c. brown sugar, packed
1/2 c. sugar
2 eggs, beaten
1 t. vanilla extract
3.4-oz. pkg. instant vanilla pudding mix
2 c. all-purpose flour
1 c. quick-cooking oats, uncooked
1 t. baking soda
12-oz. pkg. semi-sweet chocolate chips
1/4 c. chopped pecans
Optional: pecan halves

In a large bowl, beat together butter and sugars. Beat in eggs and vanilla. Add dry pudding mix, flour, oats and baking soda; mix just until well blended. Fold in chocolate chips and nuts. Drop by tablespoonfuls onto greased baking sheets. Top each with a pecan half if desired. Bake at 350 degrees for 12 to 14 minutes.

★ KITCHEN TIP ★ After baking and cooling, freeze these cookies on paper plates covered with a plastic bag and they will keep their shape. Freeze for up to 3 months.

Favorite Chocolate Chippers

MENU 5

Tina Goodpasture, Meadowview, VA

Grilled Ham Panini

Treat yourself to this fast-fix sandwich on a busy night. A griddle or panini press works great for this yummy sandwich!

Makes one sandwich

2 slices sourdough bread
1 T. mayonnaise
6 slices deli smoked ham
2 slices tomato
1 slice Cheddar cheese

Spread both slices of bread with mayonnaise on one side. Top one slice with ham, tomato, cheese and remaining bread slice. Spray a griddle or skillet with non-stick vegetable spray. Place ham sandwich on griddle or in preheated panini press. Cook sandwich over medium heat for about 5 minutes, turning once, or until lightly golden on both sides.

★ MENU PLANNING TIP ★ If you don't have time to make fries to go with this quick sandwich, purchase some whole-grain chips to add the crunch you are looking for.

MENU 5

- **Grilled Ham Panini**
- **Spicy Sweet Potato Fries**
- **Easy Apple Crisp**
- Iced Tea

Grilled Ham Panini

MENU 5

Amanda Carew, Newfoundland, Canada

Spicy Sweet Potato Fries

Change up the sides you serve by making these sweet
potato fries with just a touch of spice. They'll love them!

Makes 4 to 6 servings

2 lbs. sweet potatoes, peeled and cut into wedges or strips
3 T. olive oil, divided
1 t. seasoned salt
1 t. ground cumin
1/2 t. chili powder
1/2 t. pepper
Optional: ranch salad dressing

Place sweet potatoes in a plastic zipping bag. Sprinkle
with 2 tablespoons oil and seasonings; toss to coat. Drizzle
remaining oil over a baking sheet; place sweet potatoes in a
single layer on sheet. Bake, uncovered, at 425 degrees for
25 to 35 minutes, turning halfway through cooking time,
until sweet potatoes are golden. Serve with salad dressing
for dipping if desired.

Spicy Sweet Potato Fries

Easy Apple Crisp

Nancy Willis, Farmington Hills, MI

Easy Apple Crisp

Garnish with a dollop of whipped cream and a dusting of cinnamon... yummy!

Serves 12 to 14

4 c. apples, cored and sliced
1/2 c. brown sugar, packed
1/2 c. quick-cooking oats, uncooked
1/3 c. all-purpose flour
3/4 t. cinnamon
1/4 c. butter
Garnish: whipped cream, cinnamon, apple slice

Arrange apple slices in a greased 11"x8" baking pan; set aside. Combine remaining ingredients; stir until crumbly and sprinkle over apples. Bake at 350 degrees for 30 to 35 minutes. Garnish as desired.

MENU 6

Jen Sell, Farmington, MN

Chicken Cordon Bleu

This is a special dish I serve family & friends. It is delicious and beautiful every time.

Makes 4 servings

4 4-oz. boneless, skinless chicken breasts
2 slices deli ham, cut in half
2 slices Swiss cheese, cut in half
1 egg, beaten
1/2 c. milk
1/4 c. dry bread crumbs
1/2 t. garlic powder
1 t. dried oregano
2 T. grated Parmesan cheese

Flatten chicken breasts between 2 pieces of wax paper until 1/4-inch thick. Top each piece with a 1/2 slice of ham and cheese; roll up tightly, securing with toothpicks. In a small bowl, beat egg and milk together; set aside. In another bowl, combine bread crumbs, garlic powder, oregano and Parmesan cheese. Dip each chicken bundle in egg mixture, then in bread crumbs. Place on a greased baking sheet; bake at 350 degrees for 45 minutes.

MENU 6

- **Chicken Cordon Bleu**
- **Sesame-Asparagus Salad**
- **Coconut Cream Pie**
- Green Salad
- Ice Water

Chicken Cordon Bleu

MENU 6

Kathy Milliga, Mira, Loma, CA

Sesame-Asparagus Salad

Our family loves this salad in springtime when asparagus is fresh...it tastes terrific and is easy to prepare.

Makes 4 to 6 servings

1-1/2 lbs. asparagus, cut diagonally into 2-inch pieces
3 T. toasted sesame oil
1 t. white wine vinegar
4 t. soy sauce
2-1/2 T. sugar or honey
4 t. toasted sesame seed

Bring a large saucepan of water to a boil over high heat. Add asparagus; cook for 2 to 3 minutes, just until crisp-tender. Immediately drain asparagus; rinse with cold water until asparagus is completely cooled. Drain again; pat dry. Cover and refrigerate until chilled, about one hour. In a small bowl, whisk together remaining ingredients; cover and refrigerate. At serving time, drizzle asparagus with dressing; toss to coat.

★ KITCHEN TIP ★ Use white pepper instead of black if you want to keep the bright color of vegetables the focus. You'll get all the flavor with no visible pepper specks.

Sesame-Asparagus Salad

MENU 6

Lauren Williams, Kewanee, MO

Coconut Cream Pie

I have such fond memories of when my dad's family would all get together to eat at a local restaurant. Their coconut cream pie was one of my favorites! This is my own version.

Serves 10

2 c. milk
1/3 c. sugar
1/4 c. cornstarch
1/4 t. salt
3 egg yolks, beaten
1-1/2 c. sweetened flaked coconut, divided
2 T. butter, softened
1/2 t. vanilla extract
9-inch pie crust, baked

Combine milk, sugar, cornstarch and salt in a large saucepan; cook over medium heat until thickened, stirring constantly. Remove from heat. Place egg yolks in a small bowl. Stir a small amount of hot milk mixture into egg yolks. Pour yolk mixture back into saucepan; simmer gently for 2 minutes. Stir in one cup coconut, butter and vanilla. Pour into crust. Spread Meringue over hot pie filling; seal to edges. Sprinkle with remaining coconut. Bake at 350 degrees for 12 minutes, or until golden.

MERINGUE:
4 egg whites
7-oz. jar marshmallow creme

Beat egg whites in a bowl with an electric mixer at high speed until stiff peaks form. Add marshmallow creme; beat for 2 minutes, or until well blended.

Coconut Cream Pie

MENU 7

Celestina Torrez, Camden, NJ

Mini Ham & Swiss Frittatas

I first started making these for my toddlers as easy-to-handle mini omelets. My husband thought they would be yummy as appetizers too, so now I serve them when we're watching the big game on TV, or for a simple appetizer when we are having a fresh salad. They're still a hit with my kids too!

Makes 2 dozen

8-oz. pkg. cooked ham, diced
2/3 c. shredded Swiss cheese
1/4 c. fresh chives, chopped
pepper to taste
8 eggs, beaten

In a bowl, mix together ham, cheese, chives and pepper; set aside. Spray mini muffin cups with non-stick vegetable oil spray. Fill muffin cups half full with cheese mixture. Spoon in eggs to fill cups. Bake at 375 degrees until golden, about 13 minutes. Serve warm.

★ KITCHEN TIP ★ Keep mini pots of your favorite fresh herbs like oregano, chives, parsley and basil on a sunny kitchen windowsill...they'll be right at your fingertips for any recipe!

MENU 7

- **Mini Ham & Swiss Frittatas**
- **Beef & Snap Pea Stir-Fry**
- **Strawberry Cake**
- Fresh Fruit
- Hot Tea

Mini Ham & Swiss Frittatas

MENU 7

Sandra Sullivan, Aurora, CO

Beef & Snap Pea Stir-Fry

In a rush? Spice up tonight's dinner with my go-to recipe for healthy in a hurry! Substitute chicken or pork for the beef, if you like.

Makes 4 servings

1 c. instant-cooking brown rice, uncooked
1 lb. beef sirloin steak, thinly sliced
1 T. cornstarch
1/4 t. salt
1/4 t. pepper
2 t. canola oil
3/4 c. water
1 lb. sugar snap peas, trimmed and halved
1 red pepper, cut into bite-size pieces
6 green onions, thinly sliced diagonally, white and green
    parts divided
1 T. fresh ginger, peeled and grated
1/2 t. red pepper flakes
salt and pepper to taste
2 T. lime juice

Cook rice according to package directions. Fluff with a fork; cover and set aside. Meanwhile, sprinkle beef with cornstarch, salt and pepper; toss to coat. Heat oil in a skillet over medium-high heat. Add half of beef and brown on both sides. Transfer to a plate; repeat with remaining beef. Stir in water, peas, red pepper, white part of onions, ginger and red pepper flakes; season with salt and pepper. Cook until peas turn bright green, one to 2 minutes. Return beef to skillet; cook for another 2 to 3 minutes. Remove from heat. Stir in lime juice and green part of onions. Serve over rice.

Beef & Snap Pea Stir-Fry

MENU 7

Steven Wilson, Chesterfield, VA

Strawberry Layer Cake

Growing up in North Carolina, spring meant strawberry time, Grandma always baked this delicious cake for the Sunday night church social.

Serves 12

6-oz. pkg. strawberry gelatin mix
1/2 c. hot water
18-1/2 oz. pkg. white cake mix
2 T. all-purpose flour
1 c. strawberries, hulled and chopped
4 eggs
Garnish: fresh strawberries

In a large bowl, dissolve dry gelatin mix in hot water; cool. Add dry cake mix, flour and strawberries; mix well. Add eggs, one at a time, beating slightly after each one. Pour batter into 3 greased 8" round cake pans. Bake at 350 degrees for 20 minutes, or until cake tests done with a toothpick. Cool; assemble layers with frosting. Garnish with strawberries.

STRAWBERRY FROSTING:
1/4 c. butter, softened
3-3/4 to 5 c. powdered sugar
1/3 c. strawberries, hulled and finely chopped

Blend butter and powdered sugar together, adding powdered sugar to desired consistency. Add chopped strawberries; blend thoroughly.

Strawberry Layer Cake

MENU 8

Julie Ann Perkins, Anderson, IN

Green Goddess Bacon Salad

This salad is perfect for a main-dish salad because it has great protein in it. Green Goddess salad dressing was so popular mid-century and now it is so popular again. We never stopped serving or loving it!

Makes 6 servings

7 eggs, hard-boiled, peeled and sliced
7 to 12 slices bacon, chopped and crisply cooked
3 c. deli roast chicken, shredded
6 to 8 c. baby spinach
1 red pepper, chopped
Optional: 1 bunch green onions, sliced
Green Goddess salad dressing to taste

In a large salad bowl, combine eggs, bacon, chicken and vegetables; mix well. Pass salad dressing at the table so guests may add it to taste.

★ KITCHEN TIP ★ Using a deli chicken saves time when you need cooked chicken for a recipe. You can take it off the bone and use what you need...save the rest in the fridge for later.

MENU 8

- **Green Goddess Bacon Salad**

- **Soft Sesame Bread Sticks**

- **Chewy Chocolaty Brownies and Chocolate-Chip Oat Cookies**

- **Chai Tea**

Green Goddess Bacon Salad

MENU 8

Lynn Williams, Muncie, IN

Soft Sesame Bread Sticks

Delicious with just about any dinner, but especially with a green salad!

Makes one dozen

1-1/4 c. all-purpose flour
2 t. sugar
1-1/2 t. baking powder
1/2 t. salt
2/3 c. milk
2 T. butter, melted
2 t. sesame seed

In a small bowl, combine flour, sugar, baking powder and salt. Gradually add milk; stir to form a soft dough. Turn onto a floured surface; knead gently 3 to 4 times. Roll into a 10-inch by 5-1/2 inch rectangle; cut into 12 bread sticks. Place butter in a 13"x9" baking pan; coat bread sticks in butter and sprinkle with sesame seed. Bake at 450 degrees for 14 to 18 minutes, until golden.

Soft Sesame Bread Sticks

Chocolate Chip-Oat Cookies

Tracey Ten Eyck, Austin, TX

Chocolate Chip-Oat Cookies

This recipe was handed down to me by my mother, who is now ninety-five. She made the best homemade cookies ever!

Makes 4 dozen

1 c. butter
3/4 c. brown sugar, packed
3/4 c. sugar
2 eggs
1 t. hot water
1-1/2 c. all-purpose flour
1 t. baking soda
1 t. salt
12-oz. pkg. semi-sweet chocolate chips
2 c. long-cooking oats, uncooked
Optional: 1 c. nuts, finely chopped
1 t. vanilla extract

In a large bowl, beat butter until soft. Gradually add sugars, blending until light and fluffy. Add eggs, one at a time, beating well after each addition. Stir in hot water. In a separate bowl, mix together flour, baking soda and salt; gradually add flour mixture to butter mixture. Stir in chocolate chips, oats and nuts, if desired; mix thoroughly. Add vanilla and blend well. Drop by 1/2 teaspoonfuls onto greased baking sheets. Bake at 375 degrees for 8 to 10 minutes, until tops are golden.

**MENU
8**

Jacklyn Akey, Merrill, WI

Chocolaty Chewy Brownies

You'll love these chewy little squares of chocolate!

Makes about 2 dozen

1 c. butter, softened
2 c. sugar
4 eggs, beaten
1 c. all-purpose flour
4 1-oz. sqs. unsweetened baking chocolate, melted
1 c. chopped walnuts
Optional: powdered sugar

In a bowl, beat butter and sugar with an electric mixer on medium speed, until creamy. Beat in eggs, mixing well. Stir in remaining ingredients. Pour into a greased and floured 13"x9" baking pan. Bake at 350 degrees for 30 minutes. Cool. Dust with powdered sugar if desired. Cut into squares.

Chocolaty Chewy Brownies

Chai Tea

Linda Behling, Cecil, PA

Chai Tea

This is our favorite after-dinner tea served with a special cookie or two. I like to serve it in big cups so each person gets plenty.

Serves 20

1 c. non-fat dry milk powder
1 c. powdered non-dairy creamer
1/2 c. sugar
2 t. ground ginger
1 t. ground cloves
1 t. ground cardamom
brewed black tea

In a large bowl, combine all ingredients except tea. To serve, add 2 tablespoons of mixture to one cup of brewed tea.

MENU
9

Barbara Burke, Gulfport, MS

Lemon-Herb Chicken Salad

The lemon-herb dressing makes this chicken salad just a little different. It is really very filling and I like to make it pretty by serving it on sliced tomatoes. It's especially good with a rustic brown bread.

Serves 4 to 6

2 boneless, skinless chicken breasts, cooked
   and diced
1/4 c. mayonnaise
1/4 c. plain yogurt
1 T. fresh dill, chopped
2 t. lemon juice
1/2 t. lemon zest
1/4 t. salt

Place chicken in a serving bowl; set aside. Combine remaining ingredients; mix well and toss with chicken. Chill before serving.

★ KITCHEN TIP ★ **An easy make-ahead!**
Cook chicken the day ahead, cube it and
refrigerate. Later, stir the salad together in
no time.

MENU 9
- **Lemon-Herb Chicken Salad**
- **Swope Bread**
- **Poppy Seed Cake**
- Sliced Tomatoes
- Iced Tea

Lemon-Herb Chicken Salad

MENU 9

Dan Needham, Columbus, OH

Swope Bread

My grandmother used to make this simple batter bread. We never did find out where the name came from, but it is tasty and easy to make. Serve with a favorite chicken salad.

Makes one loaf

2 c. whole-wheat flour
1 c. all-purpose flour
1/2 c. sugar
1 t. salt
2 t. baking soda
2 c. buttermilk
Optional: 3/4 c. raisins

In a large bowl, stir together flours, sugar and salt; set aside. In a separate bowl, dissolve baking soda in buttermilk. Stir buttermilk mixture into flour mixture; beat well. Fold in raisins, if desired. Pour batter into a lightly greased 9"x5" loaf pan. Bake at 350 degrees for one hour, until golden. Cool on a wire rack.

Swope Bread

Poppy Seed Cake

Holly Curry, Middleburgh, NY

Poppy Seed Cake

The glaze drizzled over this simple cake sets it apart from other poppy seed cakes.

Serves 8 to 10

18-1/4 oz. pkg. yellow cake mix
1 c. oil
1 c. sour cream
1/2 c. sugar
4 eggs, beaten
1/4 c. poppy seed

In a large bowl, beat together dry cake mix and all remaining ingredients. Pour into a greased and floured Bundt® pan. Bake at 325 degrees for one hour, or until a toothpick inserted near the center tests clean. Turn cake out onto a serving plate. Drizzle Glaze over top.

GLAZE:
1/2 c. sugar
1/4 c. orange juice
1/2 t. almond extract
1/2 t. imitation butter flavor
1/2 t. vanilla extract

Combine all ingredients; mix well.

Jennifer Martineau, Delaware, OH

Gramma's Smothered Swiss Steak

This classic recipe is perfect for any night of the week, but I often serve it for Sunday lunch. I serve it with fresh green beans and roasted potatoes....what a treat!

Serves 6

1-1/2 lbs. beef round steak, cut into serving-size pieces
1 T. oil
1 small onion, halved and sliced
1 carrot, peeled and shredded
1 c. sliced mushrooms
10-3/4 oz. can cream of chicken soup
8-oz. can tomato sauce

Brown beef in oil in a skillet over medium heat; drain and set aside. Arrange vegetables in a slow cooker; place beef on top. Mix together soup and tomato sauce; pour over beef and vegetables. Cover and cook on low setting for 6 hours, or until beef is tender.

★ KITCHEN TIP ★ **Don't overcook fresh veggies such as green beans or broccoli. Steam them or cook them quickly in the microwave to keep their lovely color.**

MENU 10

- **Gramma's Smothered Swiss Steak**
- **Delicious Quick Rolls**
- **Mama's Cucumber Salad**
- **Strawberry-Yogurt Mousse**
- Steamed Green Beans
- Roasted Redskin Potatoes
- Coffee

Gramma's Smothered Swiss Steak

MENU 10

Ursula Juarez-Wall, Dumfries, VA

Delicious Quick Rolls

My Grandma Bohannon was the most amazing woman I know! Not a single holiday meal passed without Grandma's piping-hot rolls. We make them other times of year now because they are so easy to make.

Makes one dozen

1 c. water
1 env. active dry yeast
2 T. sugar
2 T. shortening, melted
1 egg, beaten
2-1/4 c. all-purpose flour
1 t. salt

Heat water until very warm, about 110 to 115 degrees. In a large bowl, dissolve yeast in warm water. Add remaining ingredients; beat until smooth. Cover and let rise until double in size, about 30 to 60 minutes. Punch down. Form dough into 12 balls and place in a greased muffin pan. Cover and let rise again until double, about 30 minutes. Bake at 350 degrees for 15 minutes, or until golden.

★ KITCHEN TIP ★ When making yeast breads, be sure to set the bowl in a warm place away from drafts. Your bread will rise more quickly and evenly.

Delicious Quick Rolls

Virginia Shaw, Medon, TN

Mama's Cucumber Salad

I used to take this salad to my sons' baseball award dinners and picnics. Children and adults alike always request this salad...it's cool, refreshing and very simple to make.

Makes 8 to 10 servings

2 cucumbers, sliced
1 bunch green onions, diced, or 1 red onion, sliced
   and separated into rings
2 to 3 tomatoes, diced
1/2 c. zesty Italian salad dressing

Toss together vegetables in a large bowl; pour salad dressing over all and toss to mix. Cover and refrigerate at least 3 hours to overnight.

Mama's Cucumber Salad

Strawberry-Yogurt Mousse

Michelle Sheridan, Columbus, OH

Strawberry-Yogurt Mousse

A very easy-to-make, refreshing dessert I've made for many
years...you'll love it!

Makes 10 servings

2 8-oz. cartons strawberry yogurt
1/2 c. strawberries, hulled and crushed
8-oz. container frozen light whipped topping, thawed

Combine yogurt and strawberries; mix well. Fold in
whipped topping; blend well. Spoon into cups or glasses.
Place in refrigerator for 30 minutes before serving.

CHAPTER FOUR

BUY FRESH &
Savor the Season

California Pita Sandwiches, page 154   Breakfast Berry Parfait, page 158

BUY FRESH &
Savor the Season

What is seasonal food? Seasonal ingredients are food and produce that are purchased and consumed around the time that it is harvested. For example, purchasing strawberries in the spring and apples in the fall means that those fruits will be fresher and tastier because they are in season. Of course, where you live determines what foods are grown near you and in season. Strawberries are grown in many parts of the country in spring and grapes and apples are at their peak in many places in early fall. But even if you love fall apples, and you live in Florida, the ones you get in the stores from Michigan or Washington are fresher in the fall than they are in the spring because they are picked and shipped to grocery stores right after picking. If you are lucky enough to live near cities with farmers' markets, then you can take advantage of produce that is local and at the peak of freshness because fruits and vegetables produced on local farms are often fresher, as they do not require long distances for transport. Crops picked at their peak of ripeness are also better tasting and full of flavor. Some studies have shown that fruits and vegetables contain more nutrients when allowed to ripen naturally on their parent plant rather than ripening after being picked green. So when you are planning your meals, think about what food and produce is in season and choose wisely.

Fresh Market Knowhow

- Purchase local when you can. Purchasing locally grown foods helps support local farms and ranchers. And the food is fresher because it has not been shipped for long distances.

- Find sources in your community that get food to market quickly and safely. Even if you live in the midwest, many seafood stores bring in fresh fish every day. Ask your meat or produce people where they get their meat and produce and how long it has been in the case or on the shelf.

- Ask local growers how their produce was grown. If eating organic produce is important to you, ask them about their farming practices.

- If there is a certain type of produce or meat that you want, ask the specialist in your supermarket to find it for you. They will be happy to sell what the customer wants.

- Many farmers' markets are still active into the fall and in warmer states, all year long. Take advantage of the seasonal products they have to offer, including honey and other items.

- Find out what foods are local to your area. For example, there may be a dairy or creamery nearby that you have never visited. Find out their specialty and find recipes that use those ingredients.

SPRING

Kim Breuer, Minot, ND

Kim's Specialty Salad

This salad is as tasty and good for you as it is beautiful.
Make it the centerpiece of your table!

Makes 10 servings

2 heads romaine lettuce, torn
1/2 pt. raspberries
1 avocado, peeled, pitted and diced
1 red onion, chopped
1 T. sugar
2-1/4 oz. pkg. sliced almonds
1/2 c. Poppy Seed Dressing

Toss together all ingredients except sugar, almonds
and dressing in a large bowl; gently toss. Melt sugar in a
saucepan over low heat. Immediately add almonds and toss
to coat. Remove almonds from pan and set aside. When cool,
break into pieces; add to salad. Gently toss again. Drizzle
with dressing.

POPPY SEED DRESSING:
Makes 20 servings

1/4 c. sugar
3/4 c. red wine vinegar
1/4 t. salt
1 t. ground dry mustard
1 T. poppy seed
1 t. onion, minced
3/4 c. canola oil

In a blender or food processor, combine first 6 ingredients
and process until blended. With blender on high, gradually
add in oil until blended. Makes 1-3/4 cups.

Kim's Specialty Salad

BUY FRESH & SAVOR THE SEASON

Julie Hutson, Callahan, FL

Julie's Strawberry Yum-Yum

A wonderful, lighter strawberry trifle that's a snap to put together...this recipe is a winner!

Serves 8 to 10

2 3.3-oz. pkgs. instant sugar-free
   white chocolate pudding mix
4 c. 1% milk
1 baked angel food cake, torn into
   bite-size pieces and divided
2 to 4 c. fresh strawberries, hulled,
   sliced and divided
2 8-oz. containers fat-free frozen
   whipped topping, thawed
10-oz. pkg. coconut macaroon
   cookies, crushed and divided

Beat dry pudding mix and milk with an electric mixer on low speed for 2 minutes. Chill for a few minutes, until thickened. In a large trifle bowl, layer half each of cake pieces, pudding and strawberries, one container whipped topping and half of crushed cookies. Repeat layers, ending with cookies. Cover and chill until serving time.

Janet Pastrick, Columbus, OH

Crunchy Asparagus & Pasta

Prepare this dish in a skillet and serve it right from the pan!

Makes 4 to 6 servings

5 cloves garlic, minced
2 t. red pepper flakes
2 drops hot pepper sauce
1/4 c. oil
2 T. butter
1 lb. asparagus, chopped
salt and pepper to taste
1/2 t. celery seed
1/4 c. shredded Parmesan cheese,
1/2 lb. penne pasta, cooked and
   drained

In a large skillet, sauté garlic, red pepper flakes and hot pepper sauce in oil and butter for 2 to 3 minutes. Add asparagus, salt, pepper and celery seed; sauté until asparagus is crisp-tender, about 8 to 10 minutes. Remove from heat; mix in Parmesan cheese. Pour over hot pasta; toss to coat.

Crunchy Asparagus & Pasta

BUY FRESH & SAVOR THE SEASON

Maria Gomez, El Paso, TX

Shrimp & Bean Burrito Bowls

We often serve this with warm tortillas and extra chili sauce.

Makes 4 servings

3/4 c. chicken broth
2 15-1/2 oz. cans kidney beans, drained and rinsed
1-1/2 T. butter
1/2 t. salt, divided
1/2 t. pepper, divided
1 lb. medium shrimp, peeled and cleaned
2 t. olive oil
1-1/2 T. sweet chili sauce
2 c. cooked brown rice, warmed
1 T. fresh cilantro, chopped
1 avocado, peeled, pitted and sliced
2 T. crumbled cotija cheese or shredded Parmesan cheese
Garnish: 4 lime wedges

In a large saucepan over medium heat, bring broth
and beans to a simmer. Cook for 10 minutes, stirring
occasionally. Transfer bean mixture to a bowl; add butter,
1/4 teaspoon salt and 1/4 teaspoon pepper. Mash until
smooth; set aside. Sprinkle shrimp with remaining salt and
pepper. Add oil to a skillet over medium heat. Add shrimp
and cook for 4 minutes, turning after 2 minutes. Remove
from heat; stir in chili sauce. To serve, divide bean mixture
and rice among 4 bowls. Top with shrimp, cilantro and
avocado; sprinkle with cheese. Serve with lime wedges.

Shrimp & Bean Burrito Bowls

Jill Ball, Highland, UT

Melon-Berry Bowls

I am always looking for quick, healthy and yummy breakfast ideas for my teenagers. This one has become a favorite!

Serves 2 to 4

1 honeydew melon, halved and
   seeded
6-oz. container favorite-flavor
   yogurt
1/2 c. blueberries
1 c. granola cereal

Use a melon baller to scoop honeydew into balls. Combine melon balls with remaining ingredients. Spoon into individual bowls to serve.

Bob Gurlinger, Kearney, NE

Strawberry-Banana Smoothie Breakfast Bowls

These are so easy to customize. We try different fruit combinations all the time. Strawberry-banana is still my favorite.

Makes 2 servings

2 c. frozen strawberries
2 bananas, sliced and frozen
1 c. almond milk
2 T. creamy peanut butter
1 c. fresh spinach leaves
Garnish: shredded coconut, pecans,
   blueberries, strawberries, granola,
   maple syrup

In a blender, combine all ingredients except garnish; process well until smooth. Divide between 2 bowls; garnish as desired.

★ MAKE EVERYTHING BETTER ★ Use seasonal fruits to make your breakfast smoothies. Strawberries are great in the spring and raspberries in the fall.

Strawberry-Banana Smoothie Breakfast Bowls

SPRING

Sister Toni Spencer, Watertown, SD

Sunflower Strawberry Salad

A great chilled salad...super for hot summer days!

Makes 6 servings

2 c. strawberries, hulled and sliced
1 apple, cored and diced
1 c. seedless green grapes, halved
1/2 c. celery, thinly sliced
1/4 c. raisins
1/2 c. strawberry yogurt
2 T. sunflower kernels
Optional: lettuce leaves

In a large bowl, combine fruit, celery and raisins. Stir in yogurt. Cover and chill one hour. Sprinkle with sunflower kernels just before serving. Spoon over lettuce leaves, if desired.

Susan Brees, Lincoln, NE

Tuna Seashell Salad

I took this yummy salad to a potluck party and it won 1st place!

Serves 6 to 8

16-oz. pkg. shell macaroni, uncooked
12-oz. can tuna, drained
3 eggs, hard-boiled, peeled and diced
4-oz. pkg. mild Cheddar cheese, diced
1/2 to 1 c. mayonnaise-type salad dressing
1/4 c. sweet pickle relish

Cook macaroni according to package directions; drain. Rinse macaroni with cold water; drain well. Combine all ingredients in a large serving bowl; chill.

★ MAKE EVERYTHING BETTER ★ For chilled salads, cook pasta for the shortest time given on the package, then rinse with cold water. Drain well...no mushy macaroni!

Tuna Seashell Salad

SPRING

Jennifer Gutermuth, Oshkosh, WI

Veggie, Egg & Rice Breakfast Bowls

I love eating veggies for breakfast! I use whatever is in my kitchen...red pepper, zucchini, green beans. They are all good in this bowl.

Makes 4 servings

1 T. olive oil
1 lb. asparagus, cut into bite-sized pieces
3 c. fresh spinach leaves
3 c. cabbage, shredded
1-1/2 c. cooked brown rice, warmed
1/2 c. hummus
1 avocado, peeled, pitted and diced
4 eggs
Garnish: chopped pecans, pumpkin seeds

Heat oil in a skillet over medium-high heat. Add asparagus and sauté for 4 to 5 minutes, stirring occasionally, until tender; set side. In a separate bowl, combine spinach and Honey-Mustard Dressing. Add asparagus, cabbage and rice; toss until combined. Divide spinach mixture evenly among 4 bowls. Top each with hummus and avocado; set aside. To poach eggs, fill a skillet with water and bring to a simmer over medium-high heat. Swirl water with a spoon and gently slide in each egg from a saucer. Cook until set, about 2 minutes. Use a slotted spoon to remove each egg to a bowl. Garnish as desired.

HONEY-MUSTARD DRESSING:
2 T. olive oil
2 T. lemon juice
2 t. mustard
2 T. honey
1 clove garlic, minced
salt and pepper to taste

In a small bowl, whisk together all ingredients.

Veggie, Egg & Rice Breakfast Bowls

Julie Ann Perkins, Anderson, IN

Peanut Butter French Toast

Who can resist the classic taste of peanut butter & jelly?

Serves 2

4 slices white or whole-wheat bread
1/2 c. creamy peanut butter
2 T. grape jelly
3 eggs, beaten
1/4 c. milk
2 T. butter
Garnish: powdered sugar

Use bread, peanut butter and jelly to make 2 sandwiches; set aside. In a bowl, whisk together eggs and milk. Dip each sandwich into egg mixture. Melt butter in a non-stick skillet over medium heat. Add sandwiches to skillet and cook until golden, about 2 to 3 minutes on each side. Sprinkle with powdered sugar; cut diagonally into triangles.

Gladys Kielar, Whitehouse, OH

California Pita Sandwiches

Our family loves any kind of pita sandwich. When we were in California we had this sandwich at a restaurant. When we got back, I made them for us and now we have them all the time.

Makes 2 sandwiches

1 pita round, halved and split
1 avocado, halved, pitted and sliced
1 tomato, sliced
1 slice Swiss cheese, halved
several leaves Romaine lettuce
Thousand Island salad dressing
    to taste

Fill each half of pita with avocado, tomato, cheese, lettuce leaves and dressing to taste.

California Pita Sandwiches

SPRING

Linda Picard, Newport, OR

Savory Oatmeal Bowls with Egg, Bacon & Kale

This is so warm and comforting first thing in the morning. If you like it spicy, the hot pepper sauce on the veggies makes it even better.

Makes 2 servings

2 slices bacon, diced
1 bunch kale, thinly sliced
1/2 c. tomato, diced
1 t. red wine vinegar
1/8 t. salt
1 c. cooked steel-cut oats
1/3 c. avocado, peeled, pitted and diced
1 t. olive oil
2 eggs
1/8 t. pepper
Optional: 1/2 t. hot pepper sauce

In a large skillet over medium heat, cook bacon until almost crisp, stirring occasionally. Add kale; cook for 2 to 4 minutes, until wilted. Stir in tomato, vinegar and salt. Divide oats evenly between 2 bowls. Top with kale mixture and avocado; set aside. Wipe skillet clean with a paper towel; return to medium heat. Add oil and swirl to coat. Crack eggs into skillet, one at a time; cook for 2 minutes. Cover and cook for one minute, or until whites are set. Top each bowl with one egg. Sprinkle with pepper and hot sauce, if using.

★ MAKE EVERYTHING BETTER ★ Have leftover spinach from last night's salad? Swap out the kale for spinach in these bowls. Delicious!

Savory Oatmeal Bowls with Egg, Bacon & Kale

Michelle Case, Yardley, PA

Breakfast Berry Parfait

So pretty served in simple wine glasses or champagne flutes!

Serves 2

1 c. bran & raisin cereal, divided
6-oz. container strawberry yogurt
1 c. strawberries, hulled
1/2 c. raspberries
1/4 c. blackberries

Layer half the cereal and all of the yogurt in the 2 glasses. Add berries and top with more cereal.

Jill Valentine, Jackson, TN

Homemade Vanilla Ice Cream

When I was young, we'd have what we called an "ice cream supper." We would pile in the car and head to the ice cream parlor...that really hit the spot on a hot summer night.

Serves 12

2-1/2 c. whipping cream
2 c. half-and-half
2 eggs, beaten
1 c. sugar
1/4 t. salt
2-1/4 t. vanilla extract
Optional: whole strawberries

Combine all ingredients except vanilla and optional strawberries in a heavy saucepan over medium-low heat. Cook, stirring constantly, until mixture is thick enough to coat the back of a spoon and reaches 160 degrees on a candy thermometer. Remove from heat and stir in vanilla. Set pan in an ice-filled bowl; stir. Cover and chill in refrigerator for 8 hours or up to 24 hours. Pour mixture into ice cream maker and freeze according to manufacturer's directions. Garnish with whole strawberries, if desired.

Homemade Vanilla Ice Cream

Pam James, Delaware, OH

Picnic Salad Skewers

What a fun way to pack a salad! For a meal-in-one version, slide on some cubes of Cheddar cheese and cold cuts, too.

Serves 8

8 redskin potatoes
8 pearl onions, peeled
1 green pepper, cut into 1-inch squares
1 red or yellow bell pepper, cut into 1-inch squares
16 cherry tomatoes
1 zucchini, sliced 1/4-inch thick
8 wooden skewers
Optional: 4-oz. container crumbled feta cheese

Cover potatoes with water in a saucepan; bring to a boil over medium heat. Cook 10 to 13 minutes, adding onions after 5 minutes; drain and cool. Thread all vegetables alternately onto skewers. Arrange skewers in a large shallow plastic container. Drizzle with Vinaigrette. Cover and refrigerate at least one hour, turning frequently. Sprinkle with cheese before serving, if desired.

VINAIGRETTE:
2/3 c. olive oil
1/3 c. red wine vinegar
2 cloves garlic, minced
1 T. dried oregano
1 t. salt
1/4 t. pepper

Whisk together all ingredients. Makes about one cup.

Nancie Flynn, Bear Creek Township, PA

Gram's Zucchini in a Pan

Gram used to serve this as a main dish in late summer when zucchini was plentiful.

Makes 6 servings

2 T. olive oil
1 onion, thinly sliced and separated into rings
4 to 5 sweet Italian peppers, sliced
2 zucchini, thinly sliced
2 tomatoes, diced
1 t. Italian seasoning
salt and pepper to taste
3/4 c. shredded Cheddar cheese

Heat olive oil in a skillet over medium heat. Add onion and peppers; cover and cook until soft, about 5 minutes. Stir in zucchini, tomatoes and seasonings. Cover and cook to desired tenderness. Remove from heat; stir in cheese. Cover and let stand until cheese melts; serve warm.

Gram's Zucchini in a Pan

Carla Pfall, Philadelphia, PA

Grilled Chicken Tzatziki Bowls

I've served this with grilled steak and pork as well, whatever I happen to have on hand.

Makes 4 servings

1/4 c. plain Greek yogurt
2 T. olive oil, divided
1 T. plus 1-1/2 t. red wine vinegar, divided
2 cloves garlic, minced
1/2 t. dried oregano
1 lb. boneless, skinless chicken breasts, cut into
    one-inch cubes
4 wooden skewers
3/4 t. salt
1/4 t. pepper
3 cucumbers, thinly sliced
1 c. cherry tomatoes, halved
1/4 red onion, thinly sliced
2 c. cooked quinoa, warmed
1 c. tzatziki sauce
Garnish: sliced black olives, crumbled feta cheese

In a large bowl, whisk together yogurt, one tablespoon oil, 1-1/2 teaspoons vinegar, garlic and oregano. Add chicken; stir to coat. Cover and refrigerate for one hour. Drain chicken, discarding marinade. Soak skewers in water for 10 minutes. Thread chicken pieces onto 4 skewers. Season with salt and pepper. Grill chicken over medium-high heat, turning skewers occasionally, until golden and cooked through; set aside. In a separate bowl, whisk together remaining oil and vinegar. Add cucumbers, tomatoes and onion; toss to combine. To serve, divide quinoa among 4 bowls. Top with cucumber mixture and tzatziki sauce. Garnish as desired; top each bowl with one chicken skewer.

Grilled Chicken
Tzatziki Bowls

Kelly Patrick, Ashburn, VA

Summer Squash Pie

My mother and I have used this recipe every summer when summer squash is abundant.

Makes 6 to 8 servings

3 c. yellow squash, peeled and diced
1/2 c. onion, chopped
4 eggs, beaten
1/3 c. canola oil
1 c. biscuit baking mix
1/2 c. shredded part-skim
    mozzarella cheese
1/4 t. pepper

Mix all ingredients in a bowl. Pat into a 9" pie plate lightly coated with non-stick vegetable spray. Bake at 350 degrees for 50 minutes to one hour, until set. Let stand for 10 minutes; slice into wedges. Serve warm or cold.

Vickie, Gooseberry Patch

Mexican Black Bean Burrito Bowls

This budget-friendly recipe is easy to double for a crowd.

Makes 4 servings

2 c. brown rice, uncooked
15-1/2 oz. can black beans, drained
    and rinsed
1/4 c. water
1/2 t. chili powder
1/4 t. ground cumin
1/2 t. salt, divided
1 T. olive oil
1 c. corn
1 T. fresh lime juice, divided
1/4 c. fresh cilantro, chopped and
    divided
4 c. romaine lettuce, finely chopped
1 c. crumbled queso blanco or feta
    cheese
2 avocados, peeled, pitted and sliced
1/2 c. favorite salsa
1/4 c. sour cream

Cook rice according to package directions; set aside. Meanwhile, in a saucepan over medium heat, combine beans, water, spices and 1/4 teaspoon salt; cook until heated through. Cover and remove from heat. Heat oil in a skillet over medium-high heat; add corn and cook for about 5 minutes. Sprinkle with remaining salt and one teaspoon lime juice; set aside. Transfer cooked rice to a bowl; stir in 2 tablespoons cilantro and remaining lime juice. To serve, divide beans, corn, rice, lettuce, cheese and avocado among 4 bowls. Top with salsa, sour cream and remaining cilantro.

Mexican Black Bean Burrito Bowls

Shellye McDaniel, Texarkana, TX

The Best-Ever Potato Salad

A homestyle potato salad that's just plain good!

Serves 6 to 8

4 c. potatoes, peeled, cubed and
  boiled
1 c. mayonnaise
4 eggs, hard-boiled, peeled and
  chopped
1-1/2 c. celery, chopped
1/4 c. radishes, chopped
1/2 c. green onions, chopped
1/2 t. celery seed
1 T. cider vinegar
2 t. mustard
2 T. fresh parsley, chopped
1-1/2 t. salt
1 t. pepper

Combine ingredients in a large serving bowl; mix well. Cover and refrigerate until serving.

Evelyn Moriarty, Philadelphia, PA

Vegetable Quinoa Patties

This recipe is my own, adapted from one I found online and tweaked. It has become a family favorite, especially in summertime when fresh-picked veggies are available.

Makes 6 servings

3 eggs
1/2 c. shredded part-skim
  mozzarella cheese
1/2 c. cottage cheese
1/4 c. whole-wheat flour
1 carrot, peeled and grated
1 zucchini, grated
3 T. green, red or yellow pepper,
  grated
3 green onions, finely chopped
1/2 t. ground cumin
1/4 t. garlic powder
1/8 t. salt
1/4 t. pepper
2 c. cooked quinoa
1 T. olive oil

Beat eggs in a large bowl; stir in cheeses and flour, blending well. Mix in vegetables. Combine seasonings; sprinkle over vegetable mixture and mix well. Add cooked quinoa; stir together well. Heat olive oil in a skillet over medium heat. With a small ladle, drop mixture into skillet, making 6 patties. Flatten lightly with ladle to about 1/4-inch thick. Fry patties for 4 to 5 minutes per side, until golden. Serve each serving with 3 tablespoons Dilled Yogurt Dressing.

DILLED YOGURT DRESSING:
1/2 c. plain Greek yogurt
1 cucumber, peeled and diced
3 sprigs fresh dill, snipped, or 1/2 t.
  dill weed

Stir together all ingredients in a small bowl.

Vegetable Quinoa Patties

Ronda Sierra, Anaheim, CA

BLT Pasta Salad

We just love this salad with all the flavors of our favorite sandwich.

Makes 10 servings

8-oz. pkg. elbow macaroni, uncooked
4 c. tomatoes, chopped
4 slices bacon, crisply cooked and crumbled
3 c. shredded lettuce
1/2 c. mayonnaise
1/3 c. sour cream
1 T. Dijon mustard
1 t. sugar
2 t. cider vinegar
1/2 t. salt
1/2 t. pepper

Cook macaroni according to package directions; drain and rinse in cold water. Pour into a serving bowl. Add tomatoes, bacon and lettuce; toss gently and set aside. Mix remaining ingredients together in a mixing bowl; stir well. Pour over macaroni mixture; gently toss until well coated. Serve immediately.

Larry Anderson, New Orleans, LA

Herbed Zucchini & Bowties

A beautiful dish for lunch or dinner!

Serves 4

2 T. butter
1/4 c. oil, divided
1 onion, chopped
1 clove garlic, chopped
1 green pepper, diced
3 zucchini, halved lengthwise and sliced
1 t. dried parsley
1 t. dried rosemary, crumbled
1 t. dried basil
16-oz. pkg. bowtie pasta, cooked
1/2 c. shaved Parmesan cheese

In a skillet over medium heat, melt the butter with 2 tablespoons oil. Add onion and garlic; sauté for 5 minutes. Stir in green pepper; sauté for an additional 3 minutes. Stir in zucchini and herbs; cover and cook over low heat for 5 to 8 minutes, until zucchini is tender. Add remaining oil; toss with bowties. Sprinkle with Parmesan cheese.

Herbed Zucchini & Bowties

Angie Cornelius, Sheridan, IL

Summer in a Bowl

We have a large, wonderful vegetable garden every summer. This salad makes excellent use of all those peppers, cucumbers and tomatoes.

Makes 4 servings

4 roma tomatoes, seeded and
   chopped
1 cubanelle pepper, seeded
   and chopped
1 cucumber, chopped
1/4 c. red onion, minced
6 fresh basil leaves, shredded
salt and pepper to taste
4 c. Italian bread, sliced, cubed
   and toasted
3 T. olive oil

Combine vegetables, basil, salt and pepper in a bowl. Let stand at room temperature for 30 minutes. At serving time, stir in bread cubes; drizzle with oil. Mix thoroughly; serve at room temperature.

Jackie Flaherty, Saint Paul, MN

Last Hurrah of Summer Raspberry Bread

Every late August, I'd take the kids to our family cabin in Minnesota for one last week of freedom. On the way home, we'd stop at the small town market and buy raspberries to make this yummy bread.

Makes 2 regular or 4 small loaves

3 c. all-purpose flour
2 c. sugar
1-1/2 t. salt
1 t. baking soda
4 eggs, beaten
1 c. oil
2 t. almond extract
1 t. vanilla extract
3 to 4 c. raspberries
Optional: 1 c. chopped nuts

Combine flour, sugar, salt and baking soda in a large bowl; mix well. Add eggs and oil; stir just until moistened. Stir in extracts, peaches and nuts, if desired. Spread into 2 greased 9"x5" or 4, 7"x4" loaf pans. For regular pans, bake at 350 degrees for about 50 minutes to one hour. For small pans, bake for 35 minutes, or until a toothpick inserted in center comes out clean. Cool in pans for 10 to 15 minutes; remove from pans. Cool completely. Wrap in wax paper and then aluminum foil.

Last Hurrah of Summer Raspberry Bread

SUMMER

Tabetha Moore, New Braunfels, TX

Super-Easy Stuffed Peppers

My husband loves these peppers!

Serves 4

4 green, red or orange peppers, tops
   removed
1 lb. ground beef
1 onion, diced
1 T. Italian seasoning
1 clove garlic, pressed
3 c. cooked brown rice
26-oz. can spaghetti sauce, divided
salt and pepper to taste
Garnish: shredded Parmesan cheese

Bring a large saucepan of water to
a boil; add peppers and boil until
tender. Drain and set aside. Brown
ground beef with onion in a skillet;
drain. Add Italian seasoning and
garlic. Set aside 1/2 cup spaghetti
sauce. Combine ground beef mixture,
remaining sauce, cooked rice, salt

and pepper in a bowl. Arrange
peppers in a lightly greased
8"x8" baking pan. Fill peppers
completely with ground beef
mixture, spooning any extra mixture
between peppers. Top with reserved
sauce. Add pepper tops if using.
Lightly cover with aluminum foil;
bake at 400 degrees for 20 to
25 minutes. Sprinkle with
Parmesan cheese.

Sonya Labbe, Santa Monica, CA

Tomato-Basil Couscous Salad

Everyone seems to love this salad.
I think it is the combination of the
couscous, basil and tomatoes.

Makes 6 servings

2 c. water
1-1/2 c. couscous, uncooked
1 c. tomatoes, chopped
1/4 c. fresh basil, thinly sliced
1/2 c. olive oil
1/3 c. balsamic vinegar
1/2 t. salt
1/4 t. pepper

In a saucepan over high heat, bring
water to a boil. Stir in uncooked
couscous; remove from heat. Cover
and let stand for 5 minutes, until
water is absorbed. Add remaining
ingredients and toss to mix. Cover
and chill for several hours to
overnight.

Tomato-Basil Couscous Salad

Rebekah Spooner, Huntsville, AL

Johnny Appleseed Toast

I make this special breakfast often but especially in the fall when it is apple time of year!

Makes 4 servings

4 slices cinnamon-raisin bread
1-1/2 T. butter, divided
1 Gala apple, cored and sliced
4 t. honey
1 t. cinnamon

Spread each slice of bread with one teaspoon of butter. Cover each bread slice with an apple slice; drizzle with one teaspoon honey and sprinkle with cinnamon. Place topped bread slices on an ungreased baking sheet. Broil on high for one to 2 minutes, until toasted and golden.

Dale Duncan, Waterloo, IA

Savory Barley-Mushroom Bake

A terrific meatless main or side dish that takes just minutes to put together. If time is short, bake it the night before and rewarm at dinnertime.

Makes 8 servings

2 T. butter
1 onion, diced
1 c. mushrooms, chopped
1 c. pearled barley, uncooked
1/2 c. pine nuts or slivered almonds
2 green onions, thinly sliced
1/2 c. fresh parsley, chopped
1/4 t. salt
1/8 t. pepper
2 14-1/2 oz. cans vegetable or
   chicken broth

Melt butter in a skillet over medium-high heat. Stir in onion, mushrooms, uncooked barley and nuts. Cook and stir until barley is lightly golden, about 4 to 5 minutes. Stir in green onions and parsley. Season with salt and pepper. Spoon mixture into a lightly greased 2-quart casserole dish; stir in broth. Cover and bake at 350 degrees for one hour and 15 minutes, or until barley is tender and broth has been absorbed.

Savory Barley-Mushroom Bake

Christy Neubert, O'Fallon, IL

Easy Slow-Cooker Beef Stew

My sister, Crystal, gave me this wonderful recipe. It's so yummy and easy, all you need is fruit and warm bread to make a meal.

Serves 3 to 4

1-1/2 lbs. stew beef cubes
8-oz. pkg. baby carrots
3 to 4 potatoes, cubed
10-3/4 oz. can tomato soup
10-3/4 oz. can beef broth
10-3/4 oz. can French onion soup

Place beef in slow cooker sprayed with non-stick vegetable spray. Arrange carrots and potatoes over beef. Combine soups and pour over vegetables. Cover; cook on low setting for 8 to 10 hours or high setting for 6 hours.

Julie Dossantos. Fort Pierce, FL

Autumn Morning Smoothie

Our family loves to make breakfast smoothies. After baking pie pumpkins, I decided to try making smoothies for Thanksgiving morning. They were a hit! Now we enjoy them all autumn.

Makes 2 servings

1/2 c. fresh pumpkin purée or
   canned pumpkin
3/4 c. papaya, peeled, seeded
   and cubed
2 bananas, sliced
1/2 c. low-fat vanilla yogurt
1/4 c. orange juice
4 ice cubes
1-1/2 t. cinnamon
Garnish: additional cinnamon
Optional: chopped walnuts

Add all ingredients except garnish to a blender. Process until smooth; pour into 2 tall glasses or bowls. Top each with a sprinkle of cinnamon and walnuts if desired.

BUY FRESH & SAVOR THE SEASON

Autumn Morning Smoothie

FALL

Jessica Kraus, Delaware, OH

Halloween Sloppy Joes

A staple at my house for Halloween night. Everyone loves it!

Makes 6 servings

1 lb. ground beef
1 onion, chopped
1 c. catsup
1/4 c. water
2 T. brown sugar, packed
1 T. cider vinegar
1 t. Worcestershire sauce
6 hamburger buns, split

Brown beef and onion in a skillet over medium heat; drain. Stir in remaining ingredients except buns; reduce heat to medium-low. Simmer for 25 minutes, stirring occasionally. To serve, spoon onto buns.

JoAnn, Gooseberry Patch

Cinnamon-Apple Quinoa Breakfast Bowls

This makes a hearty breakfast, but sometimes we have this for a light dinner too.

Makes 4 servings

1/2 c. quinoa, uncooked, rinsed
  and drained
1-1/4 c. almond milk

1/2 t. vanilla extract
1/4 t. cinnamon
1/8 t. nutmeg
1/8 t. salt
Optional: almond milk, maple
  syrup, chopped pecans, shredded
  coconut

Prepare Maple Roasted Apples. Meanwhile, in a saucepan over medium heat, stir together quinoa, almond milk, vanilla, spices and salt. Bring to a boil; reduce heat to low. Simmer for 10 to 15 minutes, until quinoa is cooked through and liquid has been absorbed. Remove from heat; cover and let stand for 5 to 10 minutes. Fluff with a fork. To serve, divide warm quinoa among 4 bowls; top with apple mixture. Garnish as desired.

MAPLE ROASTED APPLES:

1 T. coconut oil, melted
2 T. maple syrup
1/2 t. vanilla extract
1/4 t. cinnamon
1/8 t. nutmeg
2 Gala apples, quartered and cored

In a bowl, whisk together coconut oil and maple syrup; stir in vanilla and spices. Add apples; toss until coated. Arrange apples on a parchment paper-lined rimmed baking sheet. Bake at 375 degrees for 20 to 25 minutes, basting with pan juices once or twice, until golden. Cool slightly.

Cinnamon-Apple Quinoa Breakfast Bowls

Paula Purcell, Plymouth Meeting, PA

Pumpkin Gingersnap Ice Cream

An old-fashioned shop near us used to sell this ice cream in the fall. When the shop went out of business, I had to come up with a substitute. We think my version is even better! A great harvest dessert, especially for Thanksgiving.

Makes 6 to 8 servings

14-oz. container vanilla
    ice cream, softened
15-oz. can pumpkin
1 sleeve gingersnap cookies, crushed
Optional: whipped cream, additional
    gingersnaps, candy corn

In a large bowl, combine ice cream and pumpkin; blend well by hand. Stir in crushed cookies. Cover and freeze. If desired, garnish scoops of ice cream with a dollop of whipped cream, a gingersnap cookie and several pieces of candy corn.

Catherine Sedosky, Charleston, WV

Mom's Chili Dogs

Who can resist a good, old-fashioned chili dog?

Makes 12 servings

1 lb. lean ground beef
1 onion, chopped
1/2 c. catsup
6-oz. can tomato paste
2-1/4 c. water
3 T. chili powder
1 t. salt
12 hot dogs, cooked
12 hot dog buns

Brown ground beef until no longer pink. Combine all ingredients except hot dogs and buns in a large stockpot over medium-high heat; stir well. Cover; bring to a boil. Reduce heat to low; simmer for one to 2 hours, stirring occasionally to break up beef. To serve, spoon over hot dogs in buns.

Mom's Chili Dogs

Meri Herbert, Cheboygan, MI

Carroty Bran Muffins

These muffins have so much texture and flavor and stay moist. Keep them refrigerated after baking to keep them fresh.

Makes 1-1/4 dozen large muffins

2-1/2 c. all-purpose flour
2-1/2 c. bran cereal
1-1/2 c. sugar
2-1/2 t. baking soda
1 t. salt
2 c. buttermilk
1/3 c. applesauce
2 eggs, beaten
1-1/2 c. carrots, peeled and shredded
1 green apple, cored and chopped
1 c. sweetened dried cranberries
1/2 c. chopped walnuts
1/4 c. ground flax seed

Mix all ingredients together in a large bowl. Cover and refrigerate batter for up to 2 days, or bake right away. Fill 16 large, greased muffin cups 2/3 full. Bake at 375 degrees for 15 to 18 minutes; do not overbake. Muffins will become moister if allowed to stand for awhile.

Carroty Bran Muffins

FALL

Robin Lakin, LaPalma, CA

Herbed Roast Turkey Breast

This is too good to serve only once or twice a year!

Makes 10 servings

5-lb. turkey breast
1/4 c. fresh parsley, chopped
1 T. fresh thyme or rosemary,
    chopped
zest and juice of 1 lemon
2 tart apples, peeled, cored and
    chopped
2 stalks celery, cut into thirds
4 shallots, coarsely chopped
1 c. low-sodium chicken broth
1/2 c. dry white wine or low-sodium
    chicken broth
1 T. butter, melted
1 T. all-purpose flour

Separate skin from turkey breast with your fingers to make a pocket. Combine herbs and lemon zest in a small bowl; rub under skin. Pat skin back into place. Place apples, celery, shallots, broth and wine in a 4-quart slow cooker. Place turkey skin-side up on top; drizzle lemon juice over turkey. Cover and cook on high setting for 3-1/2 to 4 hours or on low setting for 8 to 10 hours, until tender. Remove turkey from slow cooker; if desired, place in a preheated 450-degree oven 5 to 10 minutes, until skin is golden. Transfer turkey to a serving platter and keep warm. Discard apples and celery from slow cooker; pour drippings into a skillet over medium heat. Combine butter and flour in a small bowl. Whisk into drippings;cook and stir about 15 minutes, or until thickened and bubbly. Serve warm gravy with sliced turkey.

Mary Murray, Mount Vernon, OH

October Bisque

Even though I call this "October Bisque" it is good any month of the year.

Makes 8 servings

1 onion, chopped
1/4 c. butter
4 c. chicken broth
28-oz. can whole tomatoes
1 T. sugar
2 15-oz. cans pumpkin
2 T. fresh parsley, chopped
2 T. fresh chives, chopped

Sauté onion in butter until onion is tender. Add broth and simmer for 15 minutes. Place tomatoes in a blender or food processor and blend until smooth. Add tomato mixture, sugar, pumpkin, parsley and chives to broth; heat through.

October Bisque

Joyce Stackhouse, Cadiz, OH

Pumpkin Pudding

This recipe is really quick to make and scrumptious...perfect for a light dessert after a big meal. If you are watching your calories, you can use sugar-free pudding mix and skim milk.

Makes 6 to 8 servings

2 c. milk
3.4-oz. pkg. instant vanilla pudding
   mix
1 c. canned pumpkin
1 t. vanilla extract
1 t. pumpkin pie spice
1/2 t. cinnamon
Optional: whipped cream

Combine milk and dry pudding mix in a large bowl. Beat with an electric mixer on low speed for one to 2 minutes, until smooth. Add pumpkin, vanilla and spices; mix well. Spoon into individual dessert bowls; cover and chill. If desired, garnish with dollops of whipped cream at serving time.

Becky Drees, Pittsfield, MA

Trail Mix Bagels

Perfect for an on-the-go dinner, lunch or hike...a tasty energy boost!

Makes 4 servings

8-oz. pkg. cream cheese, softened
1 T. lemon juice
1/2 c. raisins
1 carrot, peeled and grated
1/3 c. trail mix, coarsely chopped, or
   sunflower kernels
4 bagels, split

Place cream cheese in a bowl. Add remaining ingredients except bagels; stir until well blended and creamy. Spread between sliced bagels.

Trail Mix Bagels

FALL

Becky Butler, Keller, TX

Apple-Walnut Chicken Salad

This tasty recipe uses the convenience of a roast chicken from your grocery store's deli...what a great time-saver!

Makes 6 servings

6 c. mixed field greens or baby greens
2 c. deli roast chicken, shredded
1/3 c. crumbled blue cheese
1/4 c. chopped walnuts, toasted
1 Fuji or Gala apple, cored and
 sliced

In a large salad bowl, toss together all ingredients. Drizzle Balsamic Apple Vinaigrette over salad, tossing gently to coat. Serve immediately.

BALSAMIC APPLE VINAIGRETTE:
2 T. frozen apple juice concentrate
1 T. cider vinegar
1 T. white balsamic vinegar
1 t. Dijon mustard
1/4 t. garlic powder
1/3 c. olive oil

Whisk together all ingredients in a small bowl.

Apple-Walnut Chicken Salad

WINTER

Amy Butcher, Columbus, GA

Ham & Potato Chowder

Crusty bread from the bakery makes this a comforting meal!

Makes 6 servings

1/4 c. butter
1 onion, chopped
3 cloves garlic, minced
1/4 c. green pepper, chopped
1/4 c. red pepper, chopped
2 carrots, peeled and diced
4 14-1/2 oz. cans chicken broth
4 c. redskin potatoes, quartered
1/4 t. nutmeg
1-1/2 t. dried thyme
2 T. all-purpose flour
2/3 c. water
2 c. milk
11-oz. can corn, drained
2 c. cooked ham, diced
oyster crackers

Melt butter in a large pot over medium heat; sauté onion, garlic, peppers and carrots until tender. Add broth, potatoes, nutmeg and thyme. Reduce heat; cover and simmer for 1-1/2 hours. Bring to a boil. Whisk flour and water together and slowly add to chowder. Boil until thickened. Remove from heat and slowly pour in milk; stir in corn and ham. Serve with oyster crackers.

Terri Lock, Carrollton, MO

Beef Porcupine Meatballs

As a teacher, I need fast homestyle meals to serve to my family of five before I leave for evening school events...this recipe is perfect.

Serves 4 to 6

8-oz. pkg. beef-flavored rice
   vermicelli mix
1 lb. ground beef
1 egg, beaten
2-1/2 c. water
cooked egg noodles

In a bowl, combine rice vermicelli mix, beef and egg, reserving seasoning packet from mix. Form mixture into one-inch balls. In a skillet over medium heat, cook meatballs, turning occasionally, until browned on all sides; drain. In a bowl, combine seasoning packet and water; pour over meatballs. Cover and simmer for 30 minutes, or until thickened and meatballs are no longer pink in the center. Serve meatballs and sauce over noodles.

Beef Porcupine Meatballs

WINTER

Sandra Sullivan, Aurora, CO

Cranberry Bread Pudding

This is the ultimate comfort food. It's a favorite fall recipe for when time is short and the oven is full. You can substitute half-and-half for the whole milk or add chopped dried apples or other dried fruits for a tasty twist.

Makes 8 servings

4 c. whole milk
4 eggs
1 c. sugar
2 t. vanilla extract
1/2 t. salt
Optional: 2 T. brandy
6 c. white bread cubes, toasted
1-1/2 c. sweetened dried cranberries
Garnish: powdered sugar, whipped topping

In a bowl, beat milk, eggs, sugar, vanilla, salt and brandy, if using. Place bread cubes and cranberries in a large slow cooker; drizzle egg mixture over bread mixture. Stir to coat evenly. Cover and cook on low setting for about 3-1/2 hours, just until pudding is set. Sprinkle servings with powdered sugar and top with a dollop of whipped topping.

BUY FRESH & SAVOR THE SEASON

Cranberry Bread Pudding

BUY FRESH & SAVOR THE SEASON

Rogene Rogers, Bemidji, MN

Pork Chops à la Orange

We love these flavors together!

Serves 6 to 8

3 lbs. pork chops
salt and pepper to taste
2 c. orange juice
2 11-oz. cans mandarin oranges,
    drained
8-oz. can pineapple tidbits,
    drained
cooked egg noodles

Sprinkle pork chops with salt and pepper; place in a slow cooker. Pour orange juice over pork. Cover and cook on low setting for 6 to 8 hours, or on high setting for 3 to 4 hours. About 30 minutes before serving, add oranges and pineapple; continue cooking just until warm. Serve with cooked noodles.

Deborah Clouser, McLean, VA

Creamy Chicken & Biscuits

You can see the smiles on the faces of my entire family when I take this dish out of the oven. It doesn't take long to make and it is so good!

Serves 8

2 c. new redskin potatoes, halved or
    quartered
2 c. carrots, peeled and sliced
1 onion, diced
3 T. butter
3 T. all-purpose flour
salt and pepper to taste
2 c. milk
1 c. chicken broth
2 cubes chicken bouillon
2 boneless, skinless chicken breasts,
    cooked and diced
12-oz. tube large refrigerated
    biscuits, cut into quarters

Cover potatoes, carrots and onion with water in a medium saucepan. Bring to a boil over medium heat; reduce heat and simmer until tender. Drain and set aside. Melt butter in another medium saucepan; stir in flour, salt and pepper, stirring constantly. Gradually add milk, broth and bouillon. Cook until thickened, about 3 to 5 minutes; set aside. Combine chicken and vegetables in a lightly greased 13"x9" baking pan. Pour sauce over top; arrange biscuits over sauce. Bake, uncovered, at 400 degrees for 15 minutes, or until biscuits are golden and sauce is bubbly.

Creamy Chicken & Biscuits

Kristine Marumoto, Sandy, UT

French Onion Soup

Makes 6 servings

If you grate your Parmesan cheese fresh right before you make this dish, you'll really taste the difference in the richness of this dish. I have the kids help me grate the cheese and they love it!

6 onions, thinly sliced
1 T. oil
4 T. butter, divided
6 c. beef broth
salt and pepper to taste
1/2 c. Gruyère cheese, shredded and divided
1/2 c. shredded Swiss cheese, divided
1/2 c. grated Parmesan cheese, divided
6 slices French bread, toasted

Cook onions in oil and 2 tablespoons butter over low heat in a 3-quart saucepan until tender; add broth. Bring to a boil; reduce heat and simmer for 30 minutes. Remove from heat; season with salt and pepper. Ladle equally into 6 oven-safe serving bowls; sprinkle each bowl with equal amounts of each cheese. Arrange one bread slice on top of cheeses. Melt remaining butter; drizzle over bread slices. Place bowls on a baking sheet; bake at 425 degrees for 10 minutes. Broil until cheeses are golden; serve immediately.

French Onion Soup

Gaynor Simmons, Hemet, CA

Spanish-Style Round Steak

Thirty-five years ago when my children were little, I put this together with what I had in my pantry. They still request it!

Serves 6 to 8

1-1/2 lbs. beef round steak or stew
    beef, cubed
2 T. olive oil
1/2 c. onion, chopped
1 clove garlic, minced
12-oz. can cocktail vegetable juice
10-1/2 oz. can beef broth
1-1/2 c. water
1-1/2 t. salt
1/4 t. pepper
1-1/2 c. long-cooking rice, uncooked
10-oz. pkg. frozen peas
1/4 c. chopped pimentos, drained

In a skillet over medium heat, brown beef in oil. Add onion and garlic; cook and stir until onion is tender. Drain; stir in vegetable juice, broth, water, salt and pepper. Bring to a boil. Cover; reduce heat and simmer 30 minutes. Add rice, peas and pimentos. Return to a boil. Cover; reduce heat and simmer an additional 20 minutes, or until rice is tender.

Cherylann Smith, Efland, NC

Herbed Sausage Quiche

This quiche is as beautiful as it is delicious! Serve for a fancy brunch or just for a special morning treat.

Serves 8

9-inch frozen pie crust, thawed
1 c. ground pork breakfast sausage,
    browned and drained
3 eggs, beaten
1 c. whipping cream
1 c. shredded Cheddar cheese
1 sprig fresh rosemary, chopped
1-1/2 t. Italian seasoning
1/4 t. salt
1/4 t. pepper
Garnish: fresh rosemary sprig

Bake pie crust according to package directions. In a bowl, mix together remaining ingredients except garnish; spread into crust. Bake, uncovered, at 450 degrees for about 15 minutes. Reduce heat to 350 degrees, cover with foil and bake for 10 more minutes or until set. Garnish with rosemary sprig. Cut into wedges to serve.

Herbed Sausage Quiche

Paige Woodard, Loveland, CO

Mocha Muffins

Using instant coffee in these muffins is easy and adds just the right amount of flavor for coffee lovers!

Makes 16 regular or 3 dozen mini muffins

2 c. all-purpose flour
3/4 c. plus 1 T. sugar
2-1/2 t. baking powder
1 t. cinnamon
1/2 t. salt
1 c. milk
2 T. plus 1/2 t. instant coffee granules, divided
1/2 c. butter, melted
1 egg, beaten
1-1/2 t. vanilla extract, divided
1 c. mini semi-sweet chocolate chips, divided
1/2 c. cream cheese, softened

Whisk together flour, sugar, baking powder, cinnamon and salt in a large bowl. In a separate bowl, stir together milk and 2 tablespoons coffee granules until coffee is dissolved. Add butter, egg and one teaspoon vanilla; mix well. Stir into dry ingredients until just moistened. Fold in 3/4 cup chocolate chips. Fill greased or paper-lined muffin cups 2/3 full. Bake at 375 degrees for 17 to 20 minutes for regular muffins or 13 to 15 minutes for mini muffins. Cool for 5 minutes before removing from pans to wire racks. Combine cream cheese and remaining coffee granules, vanilla and chocolate chips in a food processor or blender. Cover and process until well blended. Refrigerate spread until serving time. Serve spread on the side.

Mocha Muffins

Karla Neese, Edmond, OK

Savory Herb Roast

My mom would always put this roast into the slow cooker early on Sunday mornings, before getting ready for church. When we came home from church around noon, the whole house smelled wonderful! Now I make it for a special weeknight dinner!

Serves 6

3-lb. boneless beef chuck roast
salt and pepper to taste
1 to 2 T. oil
1 T. fresh chives, chopped
1 T. fresh parsley, chopped
1 T. fresh basil, chopped
1 c. beef broth
Optional: 4 to 6 potatoes, quartered; 3 to 4 carrots, peeled
    and cut into strips

Sprinkle roast generously with salt and pepper. Heat oil in a skillet; add herbs. Brown roast on all sides. Place in slow cooker; add broth. Cover and cook on low setting for 6 to 8 hours. Add potatoes and carrots during the last 2 hours of cooking if desired.

Savory Herb Roast

Debbie Donaldson, Andalusia, AL

Mrs. Palmer's Fried Chicken

This recipe brings back precious memories! Every time I fix this recipe I think of being a little girl watching my mama cook. She used the whole chicken, but I use boneless, skinless chicken breasts.

Serves 4

4 to 5 boneless, skinless chicken
    breasts
1 qt. buttermilk
salt and pepper to taste
2 c. self-rising flour
2 t. garlic powder
2 t. dried parsley
2 t. dried thyme
2 t. poultry seasoning
1 t. dried rosemary
1 t. pepper
1 qt. oil
Garnish: chicken gravy or sweet-
    and-sour sauce

Cut chicken into strips, about 3 per breast. Place chicken in a large plastic zipping bag; pour buttermilk over chicken. Seal bag and chill for 2 to 3 hours. Drain chicken, discarding buttermilk; season chicken with salt and pepper. In a separate plastic zipping bag, combine flour and seasonings; seal bag and shake to mix well. Add chicken to bag, a few strips at a time; coat thoroughly. Heat oil to 350 degrees in an electric skillet. Carefully place chicken into hot oil; cook until both sides are golden. Drain on paper towels. Serve with chicken gravy or sweet-and-sour sauce.

Mary Lou Wincek, South Bend, IN

Stuffed Pepper Soup

Make a double batch of this for game day. It keeps perfectly in a slow cooker on low setting all during the big game!

Serves 8 to 10

2 lbs. ground beef, browned and
    drained
8 c. water
28-oz. can diced tomatoes
28-oz. can tomato sauce
2 c. cooked long-grain rice
2 c. green peppers, chopped
2 cubes beef bouillon
1/4 c. brown sugar, packed
2 t. salt
1 t. pepper

Mix together all ingredients in a stockpot; bring to a boil over medium heat. Reduce heat and simmer for 30 to 40 minutes, until green peppers are tender.

Stuffed Pepper Soup

Pam Colden, Brodhead, WI

Scalloped Potatoes & Ham

This comfort food is everyone's favorite. I serve it with a green salad and some homemade bread and everyone loves it!

Serves 6

8 potatoes, peeled and sliced
1 c. cooked ham, diced
1 small onion, diced
1/2 c. shredded Cheddar cheese
salt and pepper to taste
10-3/4 oz. can cream of chicken soup

In a slow cooker, layer each ingredient in the order given, spreading soup over top. Do not stir. Cover and cook on low setting for 8 to 10 hours, or on high setting for 5 hours.

Tina Goodpasture, Meadowview, VA

Pulled Pork Sandwich

A southern-style sandwich favorite! Enjoy it like we do, served with coleslaw and dill pickles.

Serves 12

1 T. oil
3-1/2 to 4-lb. boneless pork shoulder roast, tied
10-1/2 oz. can French onion soup
1 c. catsup
1/4 c. cider vinegar
Optional: 2 T. brown sugar, packed
bread slices or rolls

Heat oil in a skillet over medium heat. Add roast and brown on all sides; remove to a large slow cooker and set aside. Mix soup, catsup and vinegar. Add brown sugar if using; pour over roast. Cover and cook on low setting for 8 to 10 hours, until roast is fork-tender. Remove roast to a platter; discard string and let stand for 10 minutes. Shred roast, using 2 forks; return to slow cooker and stir. Spoon meat and sauce onto bread slices or rolls.

Pulled Pork Sandwich

CHAPTER FIVE

PLAN-AHEAD, Make-Ahead Meals

Fresh Herb Pesto Sauce, page 222

Easy Stuffed Pepper Soup, page 247

FRIDGE & FREEZER FRIENDLY
Make-Ahead Meals

Meal time can be hectic. So when you do find time to cook, make the best of it by planning ahead and freezing meals that you can grab from the freezer and warm up in no time. Set aside a block of time that you can make multiple meals and freeze to use later. Here are some tips to make planning ahead for meals a little easier.

Make it Easy

- Use square plastic freezer containers...they take up less room in your freezer than round ones. Choose containers that hold just enough for one meal for your family.

- To make good use of space in your freezer, ladle prepared food into plastic zipping bags, seal and press flat. When frozen, they'll stack easily.

Make it Easy

- Organize your freezer so certain types of meals or other frozen items are together. Then, when it is time to find that meal, you can find it quickly and easily.

- Spend a day making double batches of favorite foods to freeze...your freezer will be full in no time.

- Pack cooked foods in plastic freezer bags or food containers, or double-wrap tightly in plastic freezer wrap or aluminum foil. Always label and date packages.

- When reheating soup or sauce on the stovetop, make sure it's at a full boil for one minute.

- Most home-cooked foods are tastiest if kept frozen no longer than 2 to 3 months.

- Cooked pastas can become mushy in the freezer. Freeze the sauce but cook the pasta fresh when it is time to serve.

- Make a batch of muffins or cookies and then place them on paper plates. Cover with a plastic freezer bag and freeze. Because they are on a plate they won't crumble or get crushed.

- Cool down hot foods before wrapping and freezing. Let just-baked casseroles stand at room temperature for 30 minutes, then chill in the fridge for 30 minutes more. Large pots of simmering soup cool quickly when set in a sink full of ice water.

- Thaw frozen foods in the fridge overnight. Cover casseroles loosely with aluminum foil and bake at 350 degrees for one hour. Uncover; bake 20 to 30 minutes longer, until hot in the center.

Julie Neathery, Oak Grove, LA

Easy Cheesy Enchiladas

Garnish with dollops of sour cream and a sprinkle of sliced green onions just before serving.

Makes 2 pans; each pan serves 6 to 8

3 lbs. ground beef
2 1-1/4 oz. pkgs. taco seasoning mix
1 to 1-1/2 c. water
16-oz. can refried beans
2 pkgs. 10-inch flour tortillas
10-3/4 oz. can cream of mushroom soup
10-3/4 oz. can cream of chicken soup
2 10-oz. cans diced tomatoes with green chiles
1-1/2 lbs. pasteurized process cheese spread, cubed

Brown ground beef in a large skillet over medium heat; drain. Add seasoning mix and water; simmer for 5 minutes. Add beans; cook for an additional 5 minutes. Spread mixture down center of tortillas; roll up. Arrange seam-side down in 2 lightly greased 13"x9" baking pans; set aside. Combine remaining ingredients in a medium saucepan. Cook over medium heat until cheese is melted; spoon over enchiladas. Cover tightly with aluminum foil and freeze, or bake at 350 degrees for 15 minutes, until bubbly.

★ HEAT & EAT ★ **Thaw overnight in refrigerator. Remove aluminum foil and follow baking instructions above, covering again if top begins to brown.**

Kathy Dean, Eau Claire, WI

Muffin Tin Meatloaves

These little gems cook up super fast, almost twice as fast as a traditional meatloaf.

Makes 12 mini meatloaves

1-1/2 lbs. lean ground beef
1 egg, lightly beaten
1 c. Italian-seasoned dry bread crumbs
1-1/2 c. zucchini, shredded
1/2 t. salt
1/4 c. catsup
Optional: dried parsley

In a large bowl, combine all ingredients except catsup and optional parsley. Mix lightly but thoroughly. Place 1/3 cup of beef mixture into each of 12 lightly greased muffin cups, pressing lightly. Spread catsup over tops. Sprinkle with dried parsley if desired. Bake at 400 degrees for 35 minutes, or until no pink remains and juices run clear.

★ HEAT & EAT ★ **Bake as directed; cool and freeze in freezer-safe containers. To serve, thaw in refrigerator for several hours to overnight. Bake at 350 degrees for a few minutes, until warmed through.**

Muffin Tin Meatloaves

Nichole Sullivan, Sante Fe, TX

Beef & Bean Burritos

The burritos are frozen individually so they are oh-so-handy for preparing just the number of servings you need.

Makes 2 dozen

1/4 c. oil
2 onions, chopped
4 lbs. ground beef
4 cloves garlic, minced
2 T. chili powder
2 t. ground cumin
salt and pepper to taste
16-oz. can tomato sauce
62-oz. can refried beans
24 10-inch flour tortillas

Heat oil in a large skillet over medium heat; cook onions until tender. Add ground beef and garlic; cook until browned. Drain; add seasonings and mix well. Stir in sauce; simmer for 5 minutes. Add beans; cook and stir until well blended. Cool slightly. Spread mixture down centers of tortillas; roll up burrito-style and arrange seam-side down on a greased baking sheet. Bake at 350 degrees for 20 minutes and serve immediately, or let cool and freeze on baking sheet. When frozen, wrap individually or in pairs and store in plastic zipping freezer bags.

★ HEAT & EAT ★ Remove wrappers and thaw desired number of burritos. Reheat on a baking sheet at 350 degrees for 15 to 25 minutes.

Beef & Bean Burritos

Pam James, Delaware, OH

Cheesy Chicken Bake

It's not necessary to thaw the frozen veggies if you're preparing this casserole to go straight into the freezer.

Serves 8

10-3/4 oz. can cream of chicken soup
1 c. sour cream
1/4 c. milk
2 c. cooked chicken, cubed
2-1/2 c. shredded Cheddar cheese, divided
3-1/2 c. frozen shredded hashbrowns, thawed
1-1/2 c. frozen peppers and onions, thawed
1-1/2 c. potato chips, crushed

Combine soup, sour cream, milk, chicken and 1-1/4 cups cheese in a large bowl. Spread 3/4 of mixture in a greased 2-quart casserole dish. Sprinkle hashbrowns, peppers and onions over top, pressing down lightly. Top with remaining soup mixture and cheese. Wrap casserole and freeze, or sprinkle with chips and bake, uncovered, at 350 degrees for 50 to 60 minutes, until bubbly. Let stand for 5 to 10 minutes before serving.

★ HEAT & EAT ★ **Thaw overnight in refrigerator. Uncover and bake at 350 degrees for 60 to 70 minutes, until bubbly. Top with chips and bake for a few minutes longer.**

Carolyn Knight, Oklahoma City, OK

Carolyn's Chicken Tetrazzini

Scrumptious made with leftover holiday turkey too.

Serves 8

2 c. sliced mushrooms
1/4 c. butter
3 T. all-purpose flour
2 c. chicken broth
1/4 c. light cream
3 T. sherry or chicken broth
1 T. fresh parsley, chopped
1 t. salt
1/8 t. pepper
1/8 t. nutmeg
3 c. cooked chicken, cubed
8-oz. pkg. spaghetti, cooked
1 c. grated Parmesan cheese

In a Dutch oven over medium heat, sauté mushrooms in butter until tender. Stir in flour. Add chicken broth; cook, stirring constantly, until sauce is thickened. Remove from heat; stir in cream, sherry or broth and seasonings. Fold in chicken and cooked spaghetti; turn mixture into a lightly greased 13"x9" baking pan. Sprinkle with Parmesan cheese. Cool; cover with aluminum foil and freeze, or bake at 350 degrees for 30 to 35 minutes, until heated through. Let stand for 5 to 10 minutes.

★ HEAT & EAT ★ **Thaw overnight in refrigerator. Uncover and follow baking instructions above.**

Carolyn's Chicken Tetrazzini

Ellen Stringer, Bourbonnais, IL

Family-Friendly Spaghetti

This recipe won an honorable mention when I entered it in a local newspaper's recipe contest. Kids love it! I've made many batches to share with new moms and their families.

Serves 10 to 12

11 c. water
16-oz. pkg. spaghetti, uncooked
1-1/2 oz. pkg. onion soup mix
.75-oz. pkg. garlic & herb soup mix
1 lb. Italian ground pork sausage
1 lb. ground beef
2 8-oz. cans tomato sauce
2 6-oz. cans tomato paste
2 T. dried parsley
2 t. dried Italian seasoning
2 t. garlic powder

Bring water to a boil in a large stockpot over medium-high heat; add spaghetti and soup mixes. Cook for 8 to 10 minutes, stirring occasionally, until spaghetti is tender; do not drain. Set aside. Brown sausage and ground beef in a large saucepan; drain. Add remaining ingredients; mix well. Add meat mixture to spaghetti mixture, stirring well. Simmer over low heat to desired consistency, 20 to 30 minutes. Serve immediately or let cool, spoon into freezer-safe containers and freeze.

★ HEAT & EAT ★ **Thaw overnight in refrigerator. Pour into a saucepan; simmer over low heat until heated through.**

Patricia Wissler, Harrisburg, PA

Freezer Taco Rice

Yummy! Add your favorite toppings like shredded cheese and sour cream to make taco salad or roll up burritos in a jiffy.

Makes 3 containers; each container serves 4 to 6

3 lbs. ground beef, turkey or chicken
3 c. onion, diced
3 1-1/4 oz. pkgs. taco seasoning mix
6 c. cooked white or brown rice
3 16-oz. cans diced tomatoes
2 12-oz. pkgs. shredded Mexican-
blend cheese

Brown meat in a large saucepan over medium heat; drain. Add onion, taco seasoning, rice and tomatoes; simmer until thickened, about 30 minutes. Cool completely. Package in 3 freezer-safe containers; freeze.

★ HEAT & EAT ★ **Thaw overnight in refrigerator. Reheat in skillet or microwave until heated through.**

Freezer Taco Rice

Terri Steffes, Jefferson City, MO

Mexican Meat Mix

Another versatile ground beef mix to keep on hand.

Makes 10 cups

4 lbs. ground beef
1 onion, finely chopped
3 c. tomato sauce
3 T. ground cumin
3 cloves garlic, chopped
salt and pepper to taste
1/2 c. fresh Italian parsley, chopped

Brown ground beef and onion in a large skillet over medium heat. Drain; add tomato sauce, cumin, garlic, salt and pepper. Stir in parsley; cook until thickened. Cool completely; package in one-cup portions in freezer-safe containers.

★ HEAT & EAT ★ **Thaw desired amount in refrigerator overnight. Use in recipes calling for browned ground beef with tomato sauce, like tacos or Tex-Mex Stuffed Peppers (page 232).**

Susan Fountain, Stanton, MI

Grandma Dumeney's Baked Beans

My Grandma Dumeney brought her sweet baked beans to every family reunion...everyone really looked forward to them! Grandma was eighty-four when she shared this simple recipe with me, and I'm so glad she did!

Serves 8

3 28-oz. cans pork & beans
1 lb. bacon, crisply cooked and
   crumbled
1 c. brown sugar, packed
1 c. catsup
1 onion, diced

Combine all ingredients in a large bowl and mix well. Transfer to a lightly greased 4-quart casserole dish with a lid. Bake, covered, at 400 degrees for one hour. Reduce temperature to 350 degrees; uncover dish and bake for an additional hour.

★ MAKE AHEAD ★ **Prepare as directed. Refrigerate until ready to bake the next day.**

Grandma Dumeney's Baked Beans

Colleen Hinker, Santa Rosa, NM

Fresh Herb Pesto Sauce

Classic pesto is made with basil and pine nuts, but try other tasty combinations, like rosemary and pecans or oregano and almonds... delicious!

Makes about 1-1/2 cups

2 c. fresh herb leaves, coarsely chopped
6 cloves garlic, chopped

1 c. nuts, chopped
1/2 c. olive oil
1/2 t. salt
3/4 c. grated Parmesan or Romano cheese

Mix herbs, garlic, nuts, oil and salt in a blender. Process until smooth, adding a little more oil if needed to make blending easier. Transfer to a bowl and stir in grated cheese. Refrigerate in an airtight container.

★ MAKE AHEAD ★ **Prepare as directed. Spoon into ice cube trays and freeze for later use in soups, salads or casseroles.**

Fresh Herb Pesto Sauce

Molly Cool, Delaware, OH

Polynesian Spareribs

Double the recipe and freeze...you'll be ready for the next game day!

Makes 4 to 6 servings

4 lbs. pork spareribs, cut into
    serving-size portions
2 onions, chopped
2 carrots, peeled and chopped
2 T. oil
1-1/3 c. pineapple juice
2/3 c. red wine vinegar
2 T. Worcestershire sauce
2 t. soy sauce
2/3 c. brown sugar, packed
2 T. cornstarch
1/2 c. water
juice and zest of 1 lemon
salt and pepper to taste

Arrange spareribs in a roasting pan; bake at 425 degrees for 20 minutes. Drain drippings from pan; set ribs aside. In a saucepan over medium heat, sauté vegetables in oil until tender. Add pineapple juice, vinegar, sauces and sugar, stirring until sugar dissolves. Simmer over low heat for 20 minutes, stirring occasionally. Combine cornstarch and water in a small bowl; stir into sauce along with lemon juice, zest, salt and pepper. Bring to a boil, stirring constantly. Reduce heat to low; simmer for 2 to 3 minutes, until thickened. Pour sauce over ribs. Bake at 350 degrees for 40 minutes, basting every 10 minutes. Serve hot, or let cool, wrap in aluminum foil and freeze.

★ HEAT & EAT ★ **Thaw overnight in refrigerator. Place in roasting pan; cover. Bake at 400 degrees for 30 minutes.**

Suzanne Morrow, Moorhead, MN

Granny's Macaroni Salad

My family loves this cheesy macaroni salad made from my grandmother's own recipe. She was a very good granny to me!

Serves 15 to 20

48-oz. pkg. macaroni shells,
    uncooked
8-oz. pkg. pasteurized process
    cheese, cubed
1 green pepper, chopped
1 cucumber, shredded
4 to 5 carrots, peeled and shredded
2 tomatoes, chopped

Cook macaroni according to package directions. Drain and rinse with cold water. In a large serving bowl, mix cheese and vegetables together; add macaroni. Toss together. Add Salad Dressing and mix well. Refrigerate 8 hours to overnight to allow flavors to combine.

SALAD DRESSING:
2 c. mayonnaise-style salad dressing
2 T. sugar
2 T. vinegar
1 T. mustard

Mix together in a small bowl.

★ MAKE AHEAD ★ **Prepare as directed. Refrigerate until ready to serve the next day.**

Granny's Macaroni Salad

Bev Westfall, Berlin, NY

Hungarian Goulash

A hearty dish that's a longtime favorite of my family. Add some green pepper along with the ground beef or spice it up with garlic, fresh parsley or oregano.

Serves 4

3/4 lb. ground beef
2 T. onion, chopped
1 c. elbow macaroni, cooked
1 c. shredded mozzarella cheese
10-3/4 oz. can tomato soup
1/2 c. Italian-seasoned dry bread
    crumbs
2 T. butter, diced

Brown ground beef and onion in a large skillet over medium heat; drain. Layer half each of macaroni, meat mixture, cheese and soup in a lightly greased 2-1/2 quart casserole dish. Repeat layers; top with bread crumbs and dot with butter. Cover tightly with aluminum foil and freeze, or bake at 350 degrees for one hour. Or, place in foil muffin cups and cover and freeze, or bake at 350 degrees for 15 minutes.

★ HEAT & EAT ★ Thaw overnight in refrigerator. Follow baking instructions above.

Hungarian Goulash

Lisa Allbright, Crockett, TX

James' Sloppy Joes

Toast the buns first...no more sogginess!

Serves 6 to 8

2 lbs. ground beef
1 onion, chopped
1/2 c. green pepper, chopped
1/2 c. celery, chopped
2 14-1/2 oz. cans stewed tomatoes
2 c. tomato sauce
1/2 c. catsup
1/4 c. brown sugar, packed
2 T. spicy mustard
1 T. Worcestershire sauce
1/4 t. salt
1/4 t. pepper
6 to 8 sandwich buns, split

Brown ground beef, onion, green pepper and celery in a large skillet over medium heat; drain. Add remaining ingredients except buns. Bring to a boil; reduce heat and simmer for one hour, stirring occasionally. Spoon onto buns and serve, or cool completely and package in freezer-safe containers.

★ HEAT & EAT ★ **Thaw overnight in refrigerator. In a saucepan, reheat over medium heat until hot and bubbly. Serve on buns.**

James' Sloppy Joes

Kristin Stone, Davis, CA

Kristin's Perfect Pizza Dough

My mom used to make this homemade pizza when I was a child and I adored it. Now I make it!

Serves 6

5 c. bread flour
1-1/2 t. salt
1 t. sugar
1-1/2 c. warm water
1-1/2 T. oil
1 env. quick-rising yeast
Garnish: favorite pizza toppings

In a bowl, combine flour, salt and sugar. Heat water until very warm, about 110 to 115 degrees. Add water to bowl along with oil and yeast; stir. Knead by hand for 3 minutes; form into a ball. Cover and let rise until double in size, about an hour. Punch down dough; let rest for 4 minutes. On a floured surface, roll out dough about 1/4-inch thick. Place on 2 ungreased 12" round pizza pans. Let rise an additional 10 to 15 minutes. Spread Pizza Sauce over dough; add desired toppings. Place in a cold oven; turn to 500 degrees. Bake for 17 to 20 minutes, until golden.

★ MAKE AHEAD ★ **Prepare dough as instructed but do not bake. Do not add Classic Pizza Sauce or toppings. Cover and freeze dough on pans until ready to use. Add Pizza Sauce and toppings and bake when ready to serve. Will keep in freezer for up to 2 months.**

CLASSIC PIZZA SAUCE:
8-oz. can tomato sauce
6-oz. can tomato paste
1-1/4 t. dried oregano
1-1/4 t. dried basil
1-1/4 t. garlic powder
1 t. salt

Stir together ingredients in a medium bowl. Spread onto Pizza Dough, add toppings and bake as directed.

★ MAKE AHEAD ★ **Make sauce as directed. Ladle into freezer container and freeze until ready to use. Will keep for up to 3 months.**

Kristin's Perfect Pizza Dough

Terri Steffes, Jefferson City, MO

Tex-Mex Stuffed Peppers

No leftover Spanish rice on hand? Just stir some salsa into plain white cooked rice.

Makes 4 servings

2 T. olive oil, divided
4 poblano peppers, halved and
    seeded
4 c. baby spinach
1 clove garlic, pressed
salt and pepper
2 c. Mexican Meat Mix, thawed (see
    page 220)
1 c. cooked Spanish rice
8-oz. can tomato sauce
8-oz. pkg. shredded Monterey Jack
    cheese

Heat one tablespoon oil in a large skillet over medium heat; sauté pepper halves until softened. Remove peppers; set aside. Heat remaining oil in skillet; sauté spinach, garlic, salt and pepper until wilted. Spoon spinach mixture into pepper halves; wrap and freeze, or place on a broiler pan and set aside. Combine meat mix, rice and tomato sauce in skillet; heat through. Spoon meat mixture over peppers; sprinkle with cheese and place under a broiler just until cheese melts.

★ HEAT & EAT ★ **Thaw peppers and meat mix overnight in refrigerator. Add rice and sauce to meat mix as directed above. In a microwave-safe dish, top peppers with meat mixture and cheese. Microwave on high setting until heated through.**

Susie Backus, Delaware, OH

Jennifer's Soy Sauce Chicken

This yummy recipe was shared with me by my good friend Jennifer. It's an easy make-ahead dish too, since it needs to be refrigerated at least four hours for the flavors to develop. Your family will love it!

Serves 6 to 8

12 to 18 chicken drumsticks
1/3 c. brown sugar, packed
1 t. dry mustard
15-oz. bottle soy sauce
1 t. garlic powder

Arrange drumsticks in a greased 13"x9" baking pan; set aside. Mix remaining ingredients in a bowl; pour over drumsticks and toss to coat. Cover and refrigerate 4 hours to overnight, turning chicken over once while marinating. Bake, uncovered, at 375 degrees for one hour and 15 minutes, or until chicken juices run clear when pierced.

★ MAKE AHEAD ★ **Prepare recipe as directed but do not bake. Cover and refrigerate until ready to bake the next day following baking instructions. Chicken should be baked within 24 hours of preparation.**

Jennifer's Soy Sauce Chicken

Marilyn Morel, Keene, NH

Quick Meatballs & Quick & Tasty Spaghetti Sauce

My husband and boys love this tasty spaghetti sauce! It makes a great Sloppy Joe sauce, too.

Serves 4 to 6

16-oz. pkg. spaghetti or other pasta, uncooked
1/4 c. onion, diced
2 t. canola oil
14-1/2 oz. can diced tomatoes
14-1/2 oz. can beef broth
garlic powder, salt and pepper to taste

Cook pasta according to package directions; drain. Meanwhile, in a large skillet over medium heat, cook onion in oil until tender. Stir in tomatoes, broth and seasonings. Bring to a boil. Reduce heat to low; cover and simmer for 10 minutes. Serve over pasta.

★ MAKE AHEAD ★ **Prepare sauce and freeze in freezer-safe containers. To serve, thaw in refrigerator; heat on stove until hot and bubbly. Serve over cooked spaghetti.**

Carolyn Magyar, Ebensburg, PA

Quick Meatballs

Make 'em ahead...they freeze well.

Makes 3 dozen

2 lbs. ground beef
1/4 lb. ground sausage
6-oz. pkg. beef-flavored stuffing mix
3 eggs, beaten

Mix all ingredients together; shape into one-inch balls. Arrange on an ungreased baking sheet; bake at 350 degrees for 30 to 45 minutes.

★ MAKE AHEAD ★ **Bake as directed; cool and freeze in freezer-safe containers. To serve, thaw in refrigerator for several hours to overnight. Bake at 350 degrees for a few minutes, until warmed through.**

Quick Meatballs & Quick & Tasty Spaghetti Sauce

Jo Ann, Gooseberry Patch

Creamy Mushroom Sauce

With this delicious sauce tucked in the freezer, you can quickly make the chicken recipes, beef stroganoff or other mushroom-sauce based meals.

Makes 8 cups

1/3 c. oil
1/4 c. all-purpose flour
3 T. butter
6 c. sliced mushrooms
3/4 c. onion, finely chopped
3/4 t. dried thyme
1/2 t. salt
1/2 t. pepper
3 c. beef broth
1/3 c. cornstarch
3 c. milk

Combine oil, flour and butter in a large Dutch oven; cook and stir over medium heat until golden. Stir in mushrooms, onion and seasonings; cook until onion is tender. Combine broth and cornstarch; add to mushroom mixture, stirring well. Add milk; stir and cook over low heat until thickened and bubbly. Cook for 2 additional minutes. Use immediately as desired, or let cool, divide into 3 plastic zipping freezer bags in 2-2/3 cup portions and freeze.

★ HEAT & EAT ★ **Thaw overnight in refrigerator. Spoon into a microwave-safe bowl. Microwave on medium-low setting, for 8 to 12 minutes, until hot, stirring once.**

Lisa Johnson, Hallsville, TX

Lisa's Chicken Tortilla Soup

This easy-to-make soup will warm their tummies on a cold, cold night.

Serves 10

4 14-1/2 oz. cans chicken broth
4 10-oz. cans diced tomatoes with green chiles
1 c. canned or frozen corn
30-oz. can refried beans
5 c. cooked chicken, shredded
Garnish: shredded Mexican-blend or Monterey Jack cheese, corn chips or tortilla strips

In a large stockpot over medium heat, combine broth and tomatoes with chiles. Stir in corn and beans; bring to a boil. Reduce heat to low and simmer for 5 to 10 minutes, stirring frequently. Add chicken and heat through. To serve, garnish as desired.

★ MAKE AHEAD ★ **Prepare as directed. Cool; do not garnish. Ladle into freezer-safe containers and freeze. To serve, thaw overnight in refrigerator. In a saucepan, simmer over medium heat until hot and bubbly. Garnish as desired.**

Lisa's Chicken Tortilla Soup

Kris Coburn, Dansville, NY

Buffalo Chicken Pizza

Hot pepper sauce is available in several flavors and heat levels... choose one that's to your liking!

Serves 4 to 6

12-inch Italian pizza crust
1/4 c. butter, melted
1/4 c. hot pepper sauce
2 c. cooked chicken, diced
1/2 c. celery, chopped
4-oz. pkg. crumbled blue cheese

Place crust on a lightly greased 12" pizza pan; set aside. Combine butter and pepper sauce; mix well. Add chicken and celery, tossing to coat. Spread chicken mixture evenly over crust. Sprinkle with cheese. Bake pizza at 450 degrees for 10 to 12 minutes, or until heated through and crust is crisp.

★ MAKE AHEAD ★ **Prepare recipe but do not bake. Cover and freeze until ready to bake following recipe instructions. Frozen pizza will keep for up to 2 months.**

Mary Jo Babiarz, Spring Grove, IL

Chili-Weather Chili

Serve with ciabatta bread and cheese for a complete meal.

Serves 4

1 lb. ground beef
2 T. onion, diced
15-3/4 oz. can chili beans with chili sauce
8-1/4 oz. can refried beans
8-oz. can tomato sauce
8-oz. jar salsa
Garnish: shredded cheese

Brown beef and onion together in a large stockpot; drain. Add remaining ingredients except garnish. Bring to a boil and reduce heat to medium; add 1/2 cup water if mixture is too thick. Cover and simmer for 30 minutes, stirring occasionally. Garnish with shredded cheese.

★ MAKE AHEAD ★ **Prepare as directed. Cool; do not garnish. Ladle into freezer-safe containers and freeze. To serve, thaw overnight in refrigerator. In a saucepan, simmer over medium heat until hot and bubbly. Garnish as desired.**

Chili-Weather Chili

Gloria Schantz, Breinigsville, PA

Saucy Meatloaf

Real old-fashioned comfort food...
serve with mashed potatoes.

Serves 6 to 8

1-1/2 lbs. ground beef
1 egg, beaten
1 c. fresh bread crumbs
1/2 c. milk
3 T. red steak sauce
1-1/4 t. salt
1/8 t. pepper
Garnish: additional steak sauce

Combine all ingredients except
garnish; place in a lightly greased
9"x5" loaf pan. Turn meatloaf out
of the pan, wrap well with foil and
freeze, or bake at 350 degrees for one
hour, brushing top with additional
sauce. Let meatloaf stand for about
5 minutes before slicing.

★ HEAT & EAT ★ **Unwrap meatloaf;
place in loaf pan as above, cover and
thaw overnight in refrigerator. Follow
baking instructions above.**

Lizzy Burnley, Ankeny, IA

Lizzy's Make-Ahead Egg Casserole

This recipe is a favorite for breakfast,
lunch or dinner. And preparing it
ahead makes it that much easier!

Serves 12

1 doz. eggs, beaten
1 c. cooked ham, diced
3 c. whole milk
12 frozen waffles, divided
2 c. shredded Cheddar cheese,
   divided

In a large bowl, beat eggs. Stir in ham
and milk. Grease a 13"x9" baking
pan. Place one layer of waffles in
the bottom of the pan. Pour half of
the mixture on the waffles. Sprinkle
with half of the cheese. Continue
layering waffles, egg mixture and
cheese. Cover and refrigerate
overnight. Uncover and bake at
350 degrees for about one hour or
until eggs are set.

★ MAKE AHEAD ★ **Prepare recipe;
cover and refrigerate until ready to bake
the next day. Bake as directed.**

Lizzy's Make-Ahead Egg Casserole

Patricia Tiede, Cheektowaga, NY

Homemade Soup Noodles

My mom always made these tender noodles for her chicken soup. She also served them tossed with butter as a hearty side dish. These can be made very quickly in your stand mixer with the dough hook. They're well worth the effort!

Makes about 6 servings

1-1/2 c. all-purpose flour
3/4 t. salt
3 large or 4 medium eggs, beaten

Combine all ingredients in a bowl; mix with a fork until dough forms. If too dry, add a few drops of water.

Knead dough several times on a floured surface; roll out until very thin. Cut dough into thin strips or squares, as desired. Lay noodles on floured surface. Bring a large saucepan of water to a boil over high heat. Add noodles; boil about 15 minutes, until noodles rise to the top and puff up. Drain; add to hot soup or toss with butter and garnish as desired.

★ MAKE AHEAD ★ Make noodles as instructed but do not boil. Let noodles dry for 4 to 5 hours until dry. Place in plastic bags and freeze until ready to use. Noodles will keep for up to 4 months in the freezer.

Homemade Soup Noodles

Juanita Lint, Forest Grove, OR

Make-Ahead Faux Lasagna

This recipe came from a 1980 North Dakota church cookbook. It is a big hit...as tasty as lasagna but without the effort. That's how the name came about!

Serves 10 to 12

16-oz. pkg. wide egg noodles, uncooked
8-oz. pkg. cream cheese, softened
1-1/2 c. cottage cheese
1 lb. ground beef
1 T. dried, minced onion
8-oz. can tomato sauce
salt and pepper to taste

Boil half the package of noodles for 5 minutes; drain. Reserve remaining uncooked noodles for another use. Arrange half the cooked noodles in a lightly greased 2-quart casserole dish. Combine cheeses in a medium bowl. Spoon cheese mixture over noodles. Arrange remaining cooked noodles on top; set aside. Brown beef and onion in a skillet over medium heat; drain well. Combine with tomato sauce, salt and pepper; spoon over noodles. Cover and refrigerate for one to 8 hours. Uncover and bake at 350 degrees for 30 minutes. Cover with aluminum foil and bake for 15 more minutes.

★ MAKE AHEAD ★ **Prepare recipe as directed except do not bake. Cover and refrigerate until the next day. Bake as directed.**

Make-Ahead Faux Lasagna

Sonya Labbe, Santa Monica, CA

Hashbrown Quiche

A hearty quiche baked in a crust of hashbrowns! Enjoy it for breakfast, or add a zesty salad and have breakfast for dinner.

Serves 4 to 6

3 c. frozen shredded hashbrowns, thawed
1/4 c. butter, melted
3 eggs, beaten
1 c. half-and-half
3/4 c. cooked ham, diced
1/2 c. green onions, chopped
1 c. shredded Cheddar cheese
salt and pepper to taste

In a cast-iron skillet, combine shredded hashbrowns and butter. Press hashbrowns into the bottom and up the sides of skillet. Transfer skillet to oven. Bake, uncovered, at 450 degrees for 20 to 25 minutes, until crisp and golden. Remove from oven; cool slightly. Combine remaining ingredients in a bowl; pour mixture over hashbrowns. Reduce oven temperature to 350 degrees. Bake for another 30 minutes, or until quiche is golden and set.

★ MAKE AHEAD ★ **After baking, cool and cut into wedges. Freeze in individual containers. To serve, thaw in refrigerator for 4or 5 hours or overnight. Warm in oven until heated through.**

Charlotte Smith, Alexandria, PA

Easy Stuffed Pepper Soup

This is a great soup for a chilly day! It's so comforting and delicious. A good way to use some leftover cooked rice too.

Makes 6 servings

1 lb. ground beef
1/2 c. onion, diced
28-oz. can diced tomatoes
1 green pepper, diced
14-oz. can beef broth
2 c. cooked rice
salt and pepper to taste
Garnish: chopped green onions

In a stockpot over medium heat, brown beef with onion; drain. Add tomatoes with juice and remaining ingredients except garnish. Reduce heat to medium-low. Simmer until green pepper is tender, about 30 minutes. Garnish with green onions.

★ MAKE AHEAD ★ **Prepare as directed. Cover and refrigerate until ready to serve the next day. Heat through before serving.**

Easy Stuffed Pepper Soup

Harriet Hughes, Wurtsboro, NY

Harriet's Potato Pancakes

These tender golden pancakes are perfect for breakfast...delicious at dinner too, garnished with applesauce or sour cream.

Makes 6 servings

1 c. all-purpose flour
2 t. baking powder
1 t. salt
2 eggs, beaten
1 c. milk
2 T. onion, grated
1/4 c. butter, melted and slightly cooled
3 c. potatoes, peeled and finely grated

In a small bowl, mix together flour, baking powder and salt; set aside. In a separate bowl, combine remaining ingredients; mix well. Stir flour mixture into potato mixture until well blended. Drop by tablespoonfuls onto a buttered cast-iron skillet over medium heat. Cook on both sides until golden.

★ MAKE AHEAD ★ **Prepare pancakes and place individually on wax-paper-lined baking sheet. Freeze. Remove from pan and put in freezer-safe containers or plastic bags and freeze. To serve, thaw in refrigerator for one hour, then heat on baking sheet until hot.**

Claire Bertram, Lexington, KY

Baked Pork Medallions

My mother-in-law makes these fantastic medallions every New Year's Day. One more reason to celebrate!

Serves 6 to 8

1/2 c. grated Parmesan cheese
.6-oz. pkg. Italian salad dressing mix
1/4 c. red wine vinegar
2 T. olive oil
2 lbs. pork tenderloin, sliced into 1-inch-thick medallions
cooked fettuccine pasta
Garnish: chopped fresh chives

In a bowl, combine Parmesan cheese and salad dressing mix. In a separate bowl, whisk vinegar and oil. Dip medallions into vinegar mixture, then into Parmesan mixture. Place in an ungreased 13"x9" baking pan. Bake, uncovered, at 375 degrees for 30 to 35 minutes, until cooked through. Serve over pasta and garnish with chives.

★ MAKE AHEAD ★ **Prepare recipe as directed except do not bake. Cover and refrigerate until the next day. Bake as directed.**

Baked Pork Medallions

Index

U.S. to Metric Recipe Equivalents

Volume Measurements

1/4 teaspoon	1 mL
1/2 teaspoon	2 mL
1 teaspoon	5 mL
1 tablespoon = 3 teaspoons	15 mL
2 tablespoons = 1 fluid ounce	30 mL
1/4 cup	60 mL
1/3 cup	75 mL
1/2 cup = 4 fluid ounces	125 mL
1 cup = 8 fluid ounces	250 mL
2 cups=1 pint=16 fluid ounces	500 mL
4 cups = 1 quart	1 L

Weights

1 ounce	30 g
4 ounces	120 g
8 ounces	225 g
16 ounces = 1 pound	450 g

Baking Pan Sizes

Square

8x8x2 inches	2 L = 20x20x5 cm
9x9x2 inches	2.5 L = 23x23x5 cm

Rectangular

13x9x2 inches	3.5 L = 33x23x5 cm

Loaf

9x5x3 inches	2 L = 23x13x7 cm

Round

8x1½ inches	1.2 L = 20x4 cm
9x1½ inches	1.5 L = 23x4 cm

Recipe Abbreviations

t. = teaspoon	ltr. = liter
T. = tablespoon	oz. = ounce
c. = cup	lb. = pound
pt. = pint	doz. = dozen
qt. = quar	pkg. = package
gal. = gallon	env. = envelope

Oven Temperatures

300° F	150° C
325° F	160° C
350° F	180° C
375° F	190° C
400° F	200° C
450° F	230° C

Kitchen Measurements

A pinch = 1/8 tablespoon

1 fluid ounce = 2 tablespoons

3 teaspoons = 1 tablespoon

4 fluid ounces = 1/2 cup

2 tablespoons = 1/8 cup

8 fluid ounces = 1 cup

4 tablespoons = 1/4 cup

16 fluid ounces = 1 pint

8 tablespoons = 1/2 cup

32 fluid ounces = 1 quart

16 tablespoons = 1 cup

16 ounces net weight = 1 pound

2 cups = 1 pint

4 cups = 1 quart

4 quarts = 1 gallon

Send us your favorite recipe

and the memory that makes it special for you!*

If we select your recipe for a brand-new **Gooseberry Patch** cookbook, your name will appear right along with it...and you'll receive a FREE copy of the book!

Submit your recipe on our website at

www.gooseberrypatch.com/sharearecipe

*Please include the number of servings and all other necessary information.

Have a taste for more?

Visit www.gooseberrypatch.com to join our Circle of Friends!

- Free recipes, tips and ideas plus a complete cookbook index
  - Get mouthwatering recipes and special email offers delivered to your inbox.

You'll also love these cookbooks from **Gooseberry Patch**!

5-Ingredient Family Favorite Recipes

America's Comfort Foods

Best Church Suppers

Best-Ever Cookie, Brownie & Bar Recipes

Best-Ever Sheet Pan & Skillet Recipes

Cozy Christmas Comforts

Delicious Recipes for Diabetics

Harvest Homestyle Meals

Healthy, Happy, Homemade Meals

Meals in Minutes: 15, 20, 30

www.gooseberrypatch.com

From our Kitchen to Yours

Our Story

Back in 1984, our families were neighbors in little Delaware, Ohio. With small children, we wanted to do what we loved and stay home with the kids too. We had always shared a love of home cooking and so, **Gooseberry Patch** was born.

   Almost immediately, we found a connection with our customers and it wasn't long before these friends started sharing recipes. Since then we've enjoyed publishing hundreds of cookbooks with your tried & true recipes. We know we couldn't have done it without our

friends all across the country and we look forward to continuing to build a community with you. Welcome to the **Gooseberry Patch** family!

Jo Ann & Vickie